Cannabis]

to Accounti

Compliance

A CEO's Competitive Advantage

By:

Brian S. Whalen, CPA

ISBN-13: 978-1-79063-988-5

1st Edition

Green Bean CFO is a Veteran Owned Business

Please check out our website www.greenbeancfo.com or reach out to info@greenbeancfo.com

Cover photo by **Matthew Brodeur**

Artwork & Layout by

Brandon "Bova" Santiago for Green Bean Marketing
www.GreenBeanMKTG.com

DEDICATION

To Blaise, and the rest of the Whalen family – shout out from a "weed book", and

…to all those trailblazers who fought the good fight when it wasn't popular, so the current generations wouldn't end up in jail for a nickel-bag. You were shunned by the corporate world that now competes with you, so this book was written to level the playing field for you.

ACKNOWLEDGMENTS

Thank you to the colleagues who I work with daily, and to the many who contributed to this project, whether through debating the subject matter or sharing research and experiences, including Steven Berley, Willie Cardinal, Bryan C., Andrew & Naomi.

Thank you to Brandon Santiago for putting the book together – and the brand, the blog posts, the logo, the social medias, yah… pretty much everything that isn't black and white text.

Table of Contents

Table of Contents

Table of Contents

ABOUT THE AUTHOR

Brian S. Whalen, CPA

Founder & CEO of Green Bean CFO

A "Cannabis CPA"?

Tattooed and occasionally cursing like a sailor (he was a sailor in the Nuclear Navy), Brian is not your typical CPA. He has no problem serving Cannabis Entrepreneurs; it's his calling. Corporate America's competitive advantage lies within their finance and accounting functions. Green Bean CFO was founded to level the playing field for industry pioneers and newcomers alike by providing them with an affordable outsourced finance/accounting department. We help you navigate the corporate landscape, survive IRS audits, maintain compliance with state regulators and absolutely minimize the taxes that cannabis touching businesses pay under the punitive § 280E tax law. Green Bean aims to add more value than we cost and leaves no stone unturned in our mission to grow your profits. We only work with those committed to taking their canna-biz to the next level.

Brian's Story

Brian left his home in New Bedford, MA after high school and served six years in the Navy (age 18-24). After an honorable discharge, he worked in the operations departments at a commercial nuclear plant until, on his 30th birthday, he decided to quit and use his G.I. Bill for education before it expired. At that time, you couldn't work 12-hour rotating shifts and mandatory overtime and attend college, as there were no decent online programs. Next, Brian returned to serving the U.S. Government operating the Hoover Dam's power plants. Vegas was too much fun, so he went on to be a Supervisor of the electric grid (115,000 Volts and higher) in the areas from Greater Boston down through Cape Cod. He was tapped to be a Project Manager with the largest utility in New England, where he oversaw a $39,000,000 capital project involving 80+ employees in three states.

Bored with the power industry and following a bachelor's in business/accounting, Brian went on to get a master's degree in (corporate) finance from Indiana University Bloomington, followed by a Master of Science in Taxation from Bentley University in Waltham, Massachusetts. He wanted to be the finance guy for a friend who was preparing to put in an application for one of the first Registered Marijuana Dispensaries in Massachusetts circa 2014, but this friend told Brian that he needed a Certified Public Accountant – so Brian went and got a CPA license and eventually started his own practice (the friend never did get his dispensary application in).

The Team

Green Bean CFO is a consortium of Cannabis Finance and Accounting professionals. Our experienced CFOs, CPAs, Attorneys, Enrolled Agents (w/ the IRS) and bookkeepers are at your service. We also have a marketing wing – Green Bean Marketing www.GreenBeanMKTG.com (see this book cover, the GreenBeanCFO.com website, blog posts, Instagram, etc.). We're a one stop solution for a budding cannabis business. Although we serve clients nationwide, our east coast division is housed about 40 miles south of Boston, while our west coast operation stems from Portland, Oregon.

Shameless Self-Promotion

"We count the beans to grow your profits."

A savvy CEO/ owner knows that a world-class Cannabis Finance and Accounting team is a necessity and a competitive advantage. There is only one right way to do cannabis accounting! Doing accrual/ cost accounting in accordance with Generally Accepted Accounting Principles (GAAP) ensures that you pay as little tax as possible, are always state compliant and IRS audit ready, and have financial statements ready for securing investors and lenders. In addition, performance metrics can be harnessed from your financials and used to set goals for operations and management.

Our CPAs/ CFOs are your trusted advisors – we will answer your calls, clean up your books, arrange/ store your records digitally, forecast your cash flow, maximize your tax deductions under § 280E and help grow your revenues, profit margins and wealth. We'll help you strategize and act as your financial liaison so that you can focus on operations. Green Bean CFO will help you build your network by making introductions to industry service providers, from extraction experts to attorneys to chemists or bankers.

Unlike typical firms we are readily available, and we do not bill you every time you call/ email. We have skin in the game; we succeed when you do. You won't need to pay a full-time staff or the associated payroll taxes and benefits for our services either. To determine if we might work well together, contact info@greenbeancfo.com or schedule a call on our website, www.GreenBeanCFO.com. For a custom cannabis website/ logo and marketing needs, see www.GreenBeanMKTG.com. Catch us on Instagram @GreenBeanCFO and @GreenBeanMKTG.

Disclaimer

The information, materials and opinions contained on our website and this book are for general information purposes only and are not intended to constitute legal or professional advice. Neither should be relied on or treated as a substitute for specific advice relevant to specific circumstances. Green Bean CFO and Brian Whalen make no warranties, representations or undertakings about any of the content of our website and this book (including, without limitation, any as to the quality, accuracy, completeness or fitness for any particular purpose of such content), or any content of any other website referred to or accessed by hyperlinks through our website and this book. Although we make reasonable efforts to update the information on our site and this book, we make no representations, warranties or guarantees, whether express or implied, that the content on our site is accurate, complete or up-to-date.

Updates

As you read this book, you will realize that tax laws are constantly changing from the acts of local, state and federal governments. Public Law no. 115-97, better known as the Tax Cuts and Jobs Act of 2017, is the greatest change to the Internal Revenue Code (aka tax code) since at least 1986. It takes time for the IRS to issue their interpretation of these changes – they still haven't issued many of the Treasury Regulations (think of this as the playbook) that will result from recent "tax reform." Then there will be additional guidance for practitioners and the public on how to apply these new regulations. The Tax Court will be booked with cases when disputes between the public and the IRS start popping up like wild fires. These court cases will take years and years if not decades to set precedents and give us the version of clarity that we will have to settle for.

There are mentions of marijuana reform at the time of this writing; however, we could not pretend to speculate on what that might entail from a tax and legal perspective. To make a long story short, due to the nature of the industry and the timing of this book, there will be a need for continuous updates. As large portions are updated, we will continue to create new versions on Amazon and in PDF format for those who purchased this book. Through 2019, we will give you all updates at no cost to you. Please write/ email us with your order number from Amazon, Nook, iTunes, etc., and we will email a copy to you at no charge. Visit our website for information on updates.

Foreword

by Steven Berley, CPA, MBA

a.k.a. "The Apothecary CFO"

The "Green Rush" is the 21st century version of the "Gold Rush," and we're in the midst of it. Having worked at major corporations such as Ford Motor Company, Enron, Koch Industries, and Shell Oil Company, and having consulted for many large companies world-wide, I will tell you that the "Green Rush" is not for the faint of heart. I have seen failures, blow-ups and shenanigans. I have seen political nightmares and great successes, directly or as an observer, and have done so worldwide.

I have traded financial derivatives for massive corporations; most believe that Wall Street-like financial derivatives are risky, scary, challenging and stressful – they are not. It is the cannabis industry that will be more challenging than the Gold Rush or trading on Wall Street.

Many incorrectly perceive cannabis as a get-rich-quick scheme and most of them will fail. This is not a Hollywood movie promising glamour, fame and fortune right around the corner. If you could sit with us for just one day you would second guess the idea that the cannabis industry is for you. The compassion we feel for you grows every day – no pun intended.

What makes this an even more challenging business is that there are onerous federal tax laws. Those laws may change when prohibition is lifted, but in the meantime a well-developed and disciplined accounting and tax program is a must. Markets, especially new ones, are very volatile and price drops are even more pronounced. Political uncertainty at the state and federal level as well as internationally ensures a roller-coaster ride for everyone. This field of dreams, of ever-growing green fields of product and cash windfalls, will prove to be an illusion for many. Without realistic expectations and the planning, partnerships, and skillsets to thrive in every aspect, this field of dreams could turn into a forest fire, resulting in financial ruin for thousands.

The potentially negative tax and financial consequences from this industry are why it is crucial to find a CPA who invests the time to really know the cannabis business, accounting and tax landscape. There are many nuances and complexities that just don't exist in any other industry. That someone will have two key characteristics:

Work ethic
Curiosity

Find someone with these two traits, and you will find successful employees and leaders. These are the people you want to surround yourself with, not amateurs.

I have personally known Brian for less than a year. I have put my reputation on a limb for only a handful of people throughout my career, but in this risk-laden cannabis space I am suggesting a lot to say that I believe in Brian's work, and doing so with my grey hair.

He puts in the work, just as he did as a nuclear operator in the Navy, and for up to 20 hours per day. We exchange calls, emails and texts at all hours of the day, discussing research and ideas as Brian shows his passion for serving cannabis clients. He brings the questioning attitude that was ingrained in him by the military to cannabis peer groups to find a deeper understanding of very technical industry aspects. He is an open book of communication, and this book is an opening for not only the cannabis CPA, bookkeeper or tax preparer, but for the cannabis CEO to learn about accounting and taxes in a digestible manner.

Addressing two audiences at once, and doing so in one book, is remarkable. This notable approach is not only refreshing but rare. It is why everyone who has invested $1 in cannabis should read this book. Hopefully the dollars you spent for this book are the first dollars you have invested in cannabis! - Steven

Part I: Introduction

CHAPTER 1 – NEXT LEVEL CANNABIS ENTREPRENEURSHIP

"Excelling in the areas where most are failing will add dollars to your bottom line and be your competitive edge." - *Green Bean CFO*

While Green Bean CFO employs a multitude of financial planning techniques to grow your profit margins, the theme of this book is to focus specifically on legally minimizing the taxes you pay while keeping you compliant with government agencies at all levels in terms of financial, accounting and tax issues. This aspect of our overall approach adds cash to your bottom line and meets the financial planning goal of avoiding penalties, fines, and paying excessive tax.

A Note on CBD

Throughout this book, CBD and THC may be read as one and the same with respect to § 280E depending upon the circumstances of the CBD's origin. We figured we should put this up front and center. Any day now (now is December 2018) the 2018 Farm Bill might pass, and it intends to legalize the cultivation of hemp in all states. In the meantime, we have a convoluted set of rules that tell us which CBD is federally legal but do not tell us whether or not legal CBD remains Schedule I and subject to § 280E. We will explain in detail that CBD is in fact Schedule I and thereby subject to § 280E unless it is subject to specific exceptions, in which case it may or may not be subject to § 280E. § 280E is in the eye of the beholder as you will see in chapter 14.

It doesn't matter if you saw on Instagram that "CBD is now legal in all 50 states" and neither will the IRS if your source of CBD is not documented to be from a federally "legal" source. Many CBD businesses are doing themselves a disservice by not understanding the regulatory landscape. Don't take us the wrong way; we know it's not your fault that there is no specific guidance from the IRS and plenty of bogus information on the internet, but we hope to clear some of that up for you. If your CBD does not fall within the specified exceptions provided by the 2014 Farm Bill and the DEA, then you will receive the same treatment as a THC business.

About this Guide

Whether you are a pioneer in the marijuana industry and doing battle within corporate America for the first time, or a seasoned entrepreneur capitalizing on the "Green Rush," you cannot ignore the unique tax, legal and accounting challenges that are exclusive to cannabis businesses.

Many cannabis company founders pour their blood, sweat and tears into their craft - safe and accessible marijuana products;

however, expertise in the cultivation, extraction, branding and delivery to the customer must be complemented with world-class finance and accounting functions. Not only is this necessary for survival, but it's a requirement if you are looking to entice investors, secure lenders, and maximize the value of your canna-business if you choose to sell it.

This book aims to keep you out of trouble with regulators and is a guide to the rules and tools you need to be aware of to establish a competitive advantage through your finance and accounting functions. Your profitability can hinge on how you navigate the punitive tax law § 280E (defined later in this book) by properly applying the tax laws for inventories. A vast majority of those in the industry are screwing this up royally, even some with "cannabis accountants." IRS and state compliance audits can lead to fines, penalties and back taxes. Worse, your business may be shut down by regulators or fail due to poor record keeping and misinterpretation of applicable laws.

This guide prepares you for the struggles of minimizing taxation and maintaining an audit-ready cannabis business. The Courts have provided their insights in recent cases that give us some guidance in how to proceed, and we touch on them in this book. We tell you why § 280E exists, when it applies, and what you can do about it. Industry best practices in bookkeeping, record keeping, and cost accounting are discussed. The need for financial statements in accordance with Generally Accepted Accounting Principles (GAAP) to pay the least tax possible and provide transparency to investors is explained.

You will walk away with a keen sense of which services you will need to not only properly count the beans but to grow your profits.

A Word of Caution

This guide does not provide you with tips on how to be "aggressive" with your tax positions or how to cut corners in complying with industry regulations. The IRS easily identifies these tactics, and neither you nor we should risk our good name to pursue ill-gotten financial gains. There are better ways to increase margins. Playing by the rules still allows us to take advantage of the legal tax deductions that are available to you by doing cost/accrual accounting and issuing GAAP financials where applicable (more on how this works throughout the book). Doing so will give you a snapshot of how your business is performing and help you with your decision-making process as well as keep you in compliance with the alphabet soup of entities that will be regulating you.

CHAPTER 2 – WHY READ THIS BOOK?

What You Don't Know Will Hurt You

This industry is taxed like no other and, judging by the tax returns we look at daily, very few tax practitioners are protecting your interests by learning and applying the nuances of the cannabis industry. If you dove in head first without regard for the unfair tax laws, you could be heading up a river with a boat and no paddle, as the pot-friendly hip-hop artists, Cypress Hill, exclaimed on in their 1991 hit song, "Hand on the Pump." Sure, you're winning Cannabis Cups, so you don't have time for accounting and taxes – just don't be surprised when a $200,000 profit turns into a loss because you didn't bother to learn, or at least hire someone else to learn how § 280E taxes you on phantom-income (money you never made) simply because you sell cannabis. You can't avoid § 280E, but we can certainly apply a Band-Aid to stop the bleeding of cash by doing proper cannabis accounting. So, just grit your teeth and power through this guide – you will at least be familiarized with the struggles you are facing, and the methods required to overcome them.

We understand that many people who buy this book will not read it through. We don't take it personally – that's just the nature of book buyers, especially book buyers presented with the choice of growing Guerrilla Glue #4 or delving into tax laws. This chapter is for those of you who bought the book, but just want an overview. Please get through the next few pages so you know where you stand when the IRS and/ or state auditors come knocking. In this chapter, we'll give you a plain English explanation of the peculiarities and challenges that you are up against, so you will have an idea of what help you should seek if you'd like to stay out of hot water and be competitive in this dynamic industry. You can't compete if you ignore any single aspect of the business, especially finance/accounting. If you think that growing the top 1% of all crops is the single key to success, the folks that some of you may refer to as "suits" will eat your lunch. If you're in a suit, not only do you have to learn the cannabis culture, but you must reprogram your business mind. The concepts that you learned throughout your career and in B-school are warped by the regulations in this industry and often counterintuitive as a result – entity selection (Part V) is one example. For a deeper understanding of the nuances, obstacles and available solutions, read on. Or simply stop here and dust this book off after you get a letter from the IRS notifying you that you are being audited. Side note: The IRS doesn't call you and leave voicemails – those are scammers.

Get Your Priorities in Order

The cannabis industry is the fastest growing, most rapidly changing, overly complex industry in America. Business by business, town by town, county by county, and state by state, the rules and regulations differ. You need to maintain a questioning attitude; ask yourself what might bite you in the rear and seek a solution before it does. The goal is to always be compliant and audit ready.

The following should be among your top priorities:

1. **TIMELY FILE YOUR TAX RETURNS AND PAY YOUR TAXES!**

   All of them! Federal and state income taxes, local taxes, sales and use taxes, excise taxes, self-employment taxes, payroll taxes, etc. (See chapter 15 for individual and corporate tax due dates, as well as quarterly tax due dates which, *hint, hint,* aren't quarterly).

   Later in the book, we'll tell you about cannabis folks who didn't, including one who is in a federal prison cell at the time of this writing for willful failure to file a tax return. Individual returns are due in mid-April, but six-month extensions are an option. Just keep in mind that if you owe the IRS, the extension doesn't grant you extra time to pay. Partnership and corporate returns are due in mid-March and are also extendable. If you are beyond these deadlines, get your taxes prepared before the IRS calculates your tax liability for you, fines you, and tacks on interest (although fines and penalties may still apply).

2. **PAY YOUR FAIR SHARE OF TAXES, BUT NO MORE!**

   This is straight out of the *Taxpayer Bill of Rights* (more on that later). Your cannabis accountant may claim to be maximizing your deductions under § 280E, but how do they or you know if they really are? Have 10 CPAs do your tax return and you'll probably have 10 different calculations of your tax liability. As my seasoned Bentley University Tax Attorney Professor (he did Mergers and Acquisitions for Bob Kraft of Gillette/ New England Patriots) said, "I don't know why they call this program a master's in science, it should be a master's in art," insinuating that applying the tax laws is more art than science. That's right; the interpretation of the tax code often lies in the eye of the beholder – and the beholder is the IRS or the U.S. Tax Court if you want to get aggressive and go that far. Given the unique obstacles of the cannabis industry (§ 280E combined w/ extra state and local taxes/ excise taxes), the difference between $100,000 in profit and break-even for a dispensary doing $1,000,000 in sales can come down to how your tax artist paints the accounting landscape. Painting within the lines (the law) is a must, but not all paint-by-number portraits are the same.

3. DOCUMENT, DOCUMENT, DOCUMENT!

Good record keeping is paramount in an emerging industry that is under the microscope. You will need to substantiate your expenses and document methods of allocating costs to your products. You will need evidence that you have all required policies and procedures in place, and that you adhere to them. You will want everything relevant to your business to be stored in one directory on the cloud, so your investors, lenders, and auditors can be given access as needed. Proper documentation is a must if you are going to produce accurate financial statements necessary to source funding, minimize taxes, make managerial decisions, and ultimately sell the business.

4. COMPLIANCE

Don't risk your business license by failing to comply with regulators! The State, IRS, and other local and federal government agencies hold the keys to your operation and can shut it down in an instant for noncompliance.

5. CASH FLOW

Keep an eye on your cash flow. If all your cash is tied up in inventory and you can't pay that electric bill, your next crop may be at risk. The electric company doesn't care if you have $3 million worth of flower sitting with a distributor.

6. CONTROLS

Auditors and investors will look to your internal controls to gauge the accuracy of your financials. With proper controls in place from customer to cash sales, there is a much greater chance you will have a profitable business. The bonus is that you will know within reason that you are not being embezzled. We will get into detail later.

CHAPTER 3 – IS ALL THIS COMPLEX ACCOUNTING WORTH THE TROUBLE?

Following the letter of the law is not optional; however, there is still a cost vs. benefit analysis that many of us consider for the simple fact that we are human. For instance, if you have the option of parking in a private parking lot for $200 to catch a World Series game, or parking on the street the same distance from the stadium, but are guaranteed to get a $25 dollar ticket, it is probably safe to say that most would prefer the ticket (assuming being towed is not part of that option). A few people will always do what is "right" (legally) regardless, but cost is a factor for most. What if the parking ticket was $175? Now parking legally looks much more attractive for just $25 more. In the cannabis industry, doing things legally and accurately is a much more attractive option than dancing around regulations to save a few bucks. You are risking the doors being closed, incurring steep penalties and fines, and having to constantly worry that regulators/ auditors are lurking around every corner.

There are hidden rewards to doing things correctly and transparently. By doing your accounting properly, you avoid paying too much in taxes, and you can sleep at night knowing your tax returns are filed on time and correctly. With solid financial statements to refer to, you will be able to prioritize the areas that need the most attention to improve your profitability. Investors and lenders will take you much more seriously, making capital raises easier when your financials are in order. You will have a better grasp on the cash flow available to pay the bills and pay yourself and your investors. If you plan on selling the business, you will certainly fetch a higher price for it by putting to rest any uncertainties around your financial condition. You will also be more respected as a business person – we all know how we are looked at when we mention that we are in the cannabis industry.

Using a conservative estimate that ignores the financial and accounting aspects of your business will cost you 10% of revenue; experts have suggested that proper cannabis accounting will result in an extra 2 – 4% of revenue in your pocket. If doing so costs you less than this, not only do you have a financial gain, but you have the intangible gains of peace of mind, a higher business valuation, and maybe some respect from those who have the nerve to doubt your ability to run a business. If you read this far, you are clearly prioritizing business matters.

The cannabis industry is rife with bookkeepers who simply don't have the knowledge or training to perform inventory/ accrual/ cost accounting in accordance with Generally Accepted Accounting Principles (GAAP), and it's also filled with tax preparers who don't properly follow the § 280E/ § 471 guidelines. Take this into consideration when you are hiring help in your finance and accounting functions. Cannabis tax and accounting is its own sport. You wouldn't expect Michael Jordan to skate in the NHL or Wayne Gretzky to be your starting quarterback, so don't expect your excellent CPA to be an expert at cannabis accounting.

Why do I Need a Cannabis CPA/ CFO?

The problem is, many excellent CPAs, attorneys and financial advisors who don't specialize in cannabis may unintentionally give you bad advice, as conventional wisdom becomes counterintuitive in the land of § 280E. Your general practitioner attorney may end up selecting the wrong entity (entities include LLC, S Corp, Partnership, Sole Proprietor, C Corp) and inadvertently stick your spouse with half of your cannabis tax liability. You could miss a ton of deductions because your CPA doesn't know how to properly identify and allocate your cannabis expenses under the rules for inventories. You may miss out on opportunities that a professional dedicated to cannabis accounting and finance might unearth for you. Cannabis experience and an extensive network of industry veterans to refer to can be invaluable.

Before we get into the technical details of this book, let's run through a little scenario to show you how we think. If you aren't following or comprehending, it's OK, that's why you will continue to read this book to understand the concepts, and either become an expert or hire a cannabis CPA/ CFO. Even if you do get it up front, you probably want to concentrate your efforts on growing, producing, marketing, branding and selling the best THC/ CBD products on earth.

As it is written, § 280E means you get zero tax deductions; however, you can effectively "write off" your Cost of Goods Sold (COGS). Your capital investment in the cannabis products that you are selling cannot be taxed thanks to the good old Constitution of the United States of America, but Congress is not so merciful when it comes to allowing deductions for income tax purposes (they have the power to tax income). Think of the price that you pay for the cannabis products you resell, or the price you pay to manufacture and/ or prepare your products for sale as COGS. This is nearly the entire grow or extraction operation, and at the dispensary this is the cost of acquiring the cannabis products and may include the overhead and activities associated with storing, packaging, and making products ready for sale.

"Trafficking" = § 280E. Trafficking is when you sell your

freshly trimmed and tested flower to retailers, or when your Budtender sells the weed to your patient/ client. You cannot deduct ("deduct" is interchangeable with "tax write-off") the salary for that Budtender when they are doing the trafficking, but you may be able to deduct the salary for the employee in the back room of your vertically aligned grow/ dispensary who is breaking down the pounds into eighths and repackaging them in those cool tuna cans with space-monkeys on them. Now think about the supervisor of both the space-monkey can man and the Budtender. Assuming this supervisor has no other duties, half of his/ her salary, benefits, etc. would be §280E and non-deductible, and the other half could be deductible with proper cannabis accounting as he/she is supervising the tin can man whose duty is to make the goods ready for sale (COGS). 50%/ 50% – simple right?

Hold on a second, what if the space-can-man is paid $15 per hour and the Budtender $12? Would you would be happy with 50%/ 50% allocated to § 280E/ COGS? Maybe not. You might use salary as the measure, in which case you could allocate 5/9 (calculated: $15/ ($15 + $12) of the supervisor's salary to COGS and 4/9 (calculated: $12/ ($15 + $12) to § 280E trafficking activities. Using reasonable and consistent methodologies for allocations in accordance with the IRS's rules gives us a bit of control over how we make allocations to COGS. You must also be able to justify the allocations with documentation, i.e., time-sheets, job descriptions, standard operating procedures, pay-stubs, etc.

Now picture the IRS Auditor doing a walk-through of your facility with you and your representative (you'll want audit representation in the form of a CPA or tax lawyer). The Budtender and space-monkey can dude are both in jeans and a tee-shirt and are bouncing between the dispensing room and back room while doing their separate duties. This probably won't fly. Perception is reality, and both may be trafficking in the eyes of the auditor. Now, envision a Budtender at the point-of-sale location with a lime-green golf shirt that has "Budtender" embroidered on it, and in the back-room, out of sight from patrons, a dude in a lab coat and hair net who is stuffing Wedding Cake (a potent strain of cannabis) into tuna cans. Now you have your COGS room, your COGS employee repackaging product, and your tax write-offs. That back-room employee reduces your taxes when he is performing this function. The supervisor's salary allocated to that employee also reduces your tax burden. The 25% of the rent and utilities for that 250 square feet of your 1,000 square foot dispensary (250/1000 = 25%) is also a deduction, and so on. We are now only scratching the surface regarding the considerations that go into planning a tax strategy for your cannabusiness. It directly impacts your bottom line. In the scenario we just glossed over, your supervisor's $60,000 salary could be a $40,000 deduction, or no deduction at all. If you're a C Corporation, which has a flat 21% federal tax rate in 2018, that is an $8,400 difference in federal taxes alone. Your $26 an hour lab coat guy should be a write-off too. You get the picture.

Does Your Accountant Know Cannabis?

Ensure your finance/ accounting department is doing cannabis accounting properly.

The only way you are allowed any reduction in taxable income is by properly allocating expenses to COGS via accrual/ cost accounting. The only way to get all available deductions if you are a cultivator or extractor (a.k.a. producer/ manufacturer) is to contemporaneously issue financial statements in accordance with GAAP.

In plain English, to be able to get all the write-offs possible for the cannabis products that you sell, you must jump through hoops like producing financials utilizing GAAP – the standards that big businesses governed by the SEC must follow when they distribute financial statements outside of the company. Financial statements are typically your balance sheet, income statement (P&L), and statement of cash flows (the statement of shareholders' equity is more prevalent in big companies). There is a rule in the tax law that lets you allocate more things to COGS (your deductions) only if you issue GAAP financial statements: things like spoilage, depreciation/ amortization, taxes, etc. Think of financial statements as a snapshot in time that shows your assets, liabilities, income, expenses, profit/ loss and cash flow among other financial metrics.

Let's say you are a grower/ cultivator, and you are issuing your March 31st financial statements. You must follow the tax laws for inventories (Internal Revenue Code § 471 is discussed later) to get your cannabis COGS into these financial statements. You need to know the status of your inventory: how much is raw materials (seeds/ clones, etc.) how much is work in progress (think growing plants), how much is finished goods available for sale (back from the lab and packaged), and how much was sold in the period. How do you accomplish this? Your state will likely dictate the seed to sale inventory system you must use (Metrc, Agrisoft, MJ Freeway, etc.), and your accountant will either be at the mercy of that inventory system's accuracy or will require a physical inventory be completed (best practice). If the inventory software does not match physical inventory, you will have to take a physical inventory at the end of each reporting period. Records of each strain must be maintained, and they must align with the time period estimated for the growth of said strain. More on this later, but for instance, let's say that you have some O.G. Bubba Kush that takes 120 days from the clone stage until it is sold to the dispensary. On March 31st, its week 7 of 9 in flower, and you need another 3 weeks to cure, dry, trim, test, package and deliver it to the dispensary. So, you are 85 days into the 120 total days required for producing your OG Bubba Kush. That's 71% complete. 71% of the costs of this crop is allocated to work-in-process (WIP) inventory for the purposes of your financial statements. What a recurring pain in the rear! This is just some of the work that your cannabis accountant will need to perform to produce GAAP financial statements and to thereby minimize your tax bill while complying with the IRS and the state.

Entrants to the legal cannabis industry have been piling in wheelbarrows of cash without even batting an eye at the onerous tax laws, only to discover years later that their accounting was done wrong and they paid way too much in taxes, never mind way too much to get their taxes filed incorrectly. Their records are often in shambles, making it hard to find investors or to sell their business. How can you sell something if you don't have the financial statements you need to arrive at a valuation for it? Maybe at a huge discount? Will you even know? Those who have failed to keep records and pay their fair share of taxes live in constant fear of audits upon realizing that they have been doing it wrong for way too long.

Let's face it, you don't want to pay a CPA or CFO when you have so many more appealing ways to reinvest in your business. Many incorrectly believe that hiring financial professionals is just another expense. This can be true if you hire the wrong ones or simply price-shop (you get what you pay for). After reading this guide, however, you will realize that in cannabis more than anywhere else, a dedicated industry professional can offer more value than they cost, turning an expense into an ROI (return on investment). You will want a CPA who supports you in every effort, from reviewing legal documents with financial implications to hooking you up with the phone number of the best extractor equipment manufacturer in the country.

Part II: The State of the Legal Cannabis Industry

CHAPTER 4 – HIGH ASPIRATIONS

"There is a difference between pioneers and settlers. Pioneers got arrows and settlers got land." – Christian Hageseth

The cannabis industry is the fastest growing industry in the United States, with $9 billion in revenues in 2017 and projections for well over $20 billion by 2021. Marijuana is legal in some form in thirty-three states and the District of Columbia. Even Utah hopped onboard, and they have some of the most restrictive alcohol laws in the United States. Eventually, the whole country will be able to seek a safe cannabis product for adult use; however, as of November 2018, medical marijuana is legal in 33 states and another ten have passed laws to allow adult recreational use. In addition, Washington D.C.'s laws allow for both. This creates well over 40 sets of unique laws without regard to local requirements or the type of business (cultivation, delivery, dispensary, laboratory, etc.). It is no wonder that there is so much confusion among owners and operators of cannabis businesses, as well as the professionals who service them. Add the federal government into the mix – IRS, DEA, FDA, Treasury, etc., and you are navigating an uncharted sea of mines in the North Atlantic Ocean aboard the RMS Titanic during World War II. No, I'm not high, but many with high aspirations are just looking at the shiny side of the coin.

The only constant in the industry is change. Regime change (from Obama's Attorney Generals to Jeff Sessions to Matthew Whittaker as acting AG) has added to uncertainty and it seems that even the IRS is struggling to expediently iron out the ramifications of the Tax Cuts and Jobs Act of 2017 (new tax laws). Add § 280E to this melting pot of seemingly random red tape, and it's no wonder that confusion in our industry is the norm. As the founder of Green Man Cannabis recently pointed out, "There is a difference between pioneers and settlers. Pioneers got arrows and settlers got land." I would venture to say that we are still in the frontier stages. But in business, without risk there can be no reward.

Table 1: Legal States

33 States* with Legal Access to Medical Marijuana	**10 States* with Adult Use Recreationa l Marijuana**	**33 States* with Legal Access to Medical Marijuana**	**10 States* with Adult Use Recreational Marijuana**
Alaska	Alaska	Montana	
Arizona		Nevada	Nevada
Arkansas		New Hampshire	
California	California	New Jersey	
Colorado	Colorado	New Mexico	
Connecticut		New York	
Delaware		North Dakota	
Florida		Ohio	
Hawaii		Oklahoma	
Illinois		Oregon	Oregon
Louisiana		Pennsylvania	
Maine	Maine	Rhode Island	
Maryland		Utah	
Massachusetts	Massachusetts	Vermont	Vermont
Michigan	Michigan	Washington	Washington
Minnesota		**Washington, D.C.*	**Washington, D.C.*
Missouri		West Virginia	

*and Washington, D.C.

Attorney General Session's Memo – January 2018

Sessions was fired shortly before this update; however, his direction remains the most recent guidance. In a January 4th, 2018 memorandum from Jeff Sessions to all U.S. Attorneys, the Attorney General rescinded friendlier Obama era policies (Ogden and Cole Memos) that provided some level of comfort to cannabis businesses operating within state laws. Sessions basically told his federal prosecutors to prosecute marijuana crimes at their discretion based on the guidance of their handbook, *9-27.000 – Principles of Federal Prosecution.* At one end of the spectrum, the U.S. Attorney's Office in Colorado immediately issued a statement that, despite the Sessions memo, it would be business as usual regarding cannabis companies operating under state law. At the other end of the spectrum, with no specific guidance, you might imagine a worst-case scenario: if you are in possession of a firearm (licensed/ legal or not) and are trafficking in drugs, the mandatory minimum prescribed by the *Principles of Federal Prosecution* is 5 years (per 18 U.S.C. § 924(c)). Uncertainty regarding federal prosecution was a reality under the Sessions memorandum – will Whittaker address legal cannabis? Or will his successor?

A Sea of Change

As of the writing of this book, the federal government's direction as it relates to state legal marijuana is as straight-forward as a bowl of spaghetti. An August 2018 Forbes article suggests that the White House is working to subvert legal cannabis. This is a contradiction of previous claims that the Trump administration would allow states to set the rules for cannabis. Is this misdirection by the Trump administration or misinformation? In the meantime, legislation is flying; the proposed *STATES Act* would amend the Controlled Substances Act so that it no longer applies to state legal cannabis. Another Senate Bill was introduced to federally legalize medical marijuana specifically for military veterans (and nobody else). This would allow the Department of Veterans Affairs (VA) to recommend and possibly prescribe the medicine. The 2018 Farm Bill, should it be enacted, will legalize industrial hemp, and thereby legalize CBD products derived from that hemp. As far as the use of these products as a dietary supplement, that depends whether the FDA blesses them off as well. As a result, Fortune 500 companies are on the sidelines waiting to pounce on CBD.

With all these developments, it is still unclear how each would be treated by the alphabet soup of bureaucracy. Will medical marijuana become federally legal but remain subject to IRC § 280E? Will it be legal for veterans first, then medical patients, then recreational users? Will recreational use always be federally illegal? Even if these laws pass, will cannabis products be rescheduled by DEA and thereby not subject to § 280E by the IRS? There are more questions than answers, so consult with your trusted advisers regularly.

The industry will continue to present unique challenges as long as marijuana remains federally illegal. Reliable banking, payroll systems, point of sale, etc. are difficult to come by. Even worse, when you do find the services you need to run your business efficiently, you often get price-gouged for the simple fact that they can, or they may change their business practices and no longer serve cannabis clients.

CHAPTER 5 – THE CONTROLLED SUBSTANCES ACT AND CANNABIS

There are three inflection points in the Controlled Substances Act (CSA) of 1970 that are of significance to the cannabis industry:

1. Schedule I or II
2. Schedule III, IV & V
3. Not Scheduled

Currently cannabis is Schedule I, the worst place to be on the 5 tiers. Without going into the details of the CSA, this is "bad" because the punitive tax laws of § 280E only apply to schedules I and II. If the DEA were to determine that cannabis had less potential for abuse than narcotics like methadone, oxycodone, morphine, opium etc., and abuse of cannabis may lead to moderate or low physical dependence or high psychological dependence, then cannabis could make it to Schedule III and § 280E would no longer apply. Drugs currently in Schedule III include Vicodin, Tylenol with Codeine, and Suboxone.

We discuss this more in the CBD chapter, but on September 27th, 2018, the DEA lowered a lone CBD containing medicine (Epidiolex) from Schedule I to Schedule V and announced that drugs with THC content below 0.1% will be considered Schedule V drugs if they have been approved by the

U.S. Food and Drug Administration (FDA). This should open the flood gates for CBD products that make it through the painstaking FDA approval process, as it is essentially the first time that the DEA acknowledged that they have medicinal value. Good luck getting them on board with THC.

To add insult to injury, alcohol and tobacco are **Not Scheduled** by the DEA. Massive corporations are front-running the possibility that CBD joins the ranks of booze and cigs. For instance, Coca-Cola, among other Fortune 500 companies eyeing the consumer demand for clean CBD, is rumored to be considering a line of CBD beverages. At least the DEA took a first step in the right direction with CBD.

Part III: Relevant Terms and Concepts

CHAPTER 6 – THE INGREDIENTS TO LEGALLY MINIMIZING CANNABIS TAXES

"Cost accounting is enemy number one of productivity." - *Eliyahu Goldratt*

Yep, the above is a real quote from an Israeli business guru. The bad news is that you've got to do accrual/ cost accounting and issue financial statements in accordance with Generally Accepted Accounting Principles (GAAP) (particularly if you're a manufacturer/ producer) to get the most after-tax profit out of your cannabis touching business. The good news is that we are going to tell you what these terms mean in the chapter that follows and then how the associated concepts are applied throughout the book. More good news – you can hire someone else to do this tedious, painstaking work (like Green Bean CFO)!

Let's highlight some key terms and concepts that you will become familiar with and why they matter. The following chapter includes those terms and concepts which are interrelated for the purposes of cannabis accounting. We will elaborate on these ideas throughout the book, so consider this a primer. We aren't trying to familiarize you with the jargon of a CPA, and to 99% of CPAs, these terms and concepts are not the most pertinent to the clients they serve. We are only concerned with the terms most relevant to your role in a cannabis business in Chapter 5. At the end of this chapter we'll tell you a bit more about what the squiggly "§" lines mean and quickly summarize different parts of the tax laws/ regulations.

Cannabis Touching

"Cannabis touching" is the term we will use for businesses that dispense, manufacture, cultivate, or otherwise physically touch cannabis in its Schedule I drug form (as defined by the DEA). Cannabis touching businesses that sell (aka traffic) their cannabis derived products are subject to § 280E (as opposed to a testing laboratory that does not sell/ manufacture/ cultivate cannabis and is not subject to § 280E).

Cost Accounting

Cost accounting is a detailed method for reporting the cost of manufacturing goods and performing services in the aggregate. In the cannabis space, cost accounting is the mechanism we must use to allocate costs into inventory, so when the inventory is sold, we can get the equivalent of a deduction for COGS (Cost of Goods Sold). Properly capitalizing costs to inventory via § 471 is the way you minimize your taxes under § 280E.

Capitalization

Capitalization means to account for the costs that go into the purchase or manufacturing of your cannabis products by tying them to your physical cannabis inventory, so that you can expense the costs of that inventory only when it is sold.

COGS (Cost of Goods Sold)

COGS is the capital that you put into the products that you sell; it's most of the direct and indirect costs to manufacture, cultivate, or acquire cannabis ready to sell in the dispensary. Since Congress cannot tax the return to you of that capital, COGS is your only effective deduction (§ 280E disallows all deductions).

Method of Accounting

There are little check boxes on the various types of IRS business tax return forms where you can check off either "*cash,*" "*accrual*" or "*other (specify).*" Be aware that the significance of the checkmark here is much larger than the boxes themselves!

- Cash Method – Your business deducts its expenses in the year you pay them, and records revenue on the books when the cash is credited to your account or made available to you without restriction. If you pay expenses in advance for the year, such as a 1-year insurance premium, that is still acceptable under the cash method of accounting under the 12-month rule. Beyond 12 months, you must accrue the expense.

- Accrual Method – Under an accrual method of accounting, you generally report income in the year it is earned and deduct or capitalize expenses in the year incurred. The purpose of an accrual method of accounting is to match income and expenses in the correct year.

- Hybrid Method (*aka "other"*) – As you may guess, this is a combination of the above methods of accounting and may entail other special methods in combination if they clearly reflect income, are done consistently, and aren't subject to certain restrictions.

The general rule is that, "taxable income shall be computed under the method of accounting on the basis of which the taxpayer regularly computes his income in keeping his books." Of course, the code throws curveballs such as exceptions to the general rules and gives us specific limitations on when the cash method can be used. In addition to this, the code provides that the IRS gets to ultimately decide which method clearly reflects income. Two factors will almost always point us toward the accrual method of accounting:

1. Due to § 280E, which allows us to only recognize the COGS upon the actual sale of the cannabis product, and

in order to clearly reflect income in this manner, you would have to accrue your expenses and match them to your sales. By "match," we mean at the same time.

2. Generally, when inventories are necessary, and the purchase or sale of merchandise is an income producing factor, you are required to follow Reg. § 1. 471-1 which requires the accrual method of accounting. There are exceptions to this, and particularly for qualifying small business taxpayers; however, following the rules for inventories (all the § 471 stuff) is the only way to minimize your taxes under § 280E as you will see later.

IMPORTANT: If you haven't been implementing the appropriate or required method of accounting and need to change it, you must secure permission from the IRS to do so. If you rack up penalties and fines due to changing methods without consent, you will not be forgiven by the IRS for not knowing you needed consent.

GAAP (Generally Accepted Accounting Principles)

For our purposes, cannabis producing/ manufacturing businesses that wish to minimize taxes are specifically directed by the tax code to issue financial statements in accordance with GAAP in order to allocate certain costs to COGS (those costs listed in § 1.471-11(c)(2)(iii)). GAAP is an AICPA (American Institute of Certified Public Accountants) established a set of standards, conventions and rules that accountants follow in recording and summarizing transactions and in preparing financial statements. Investors and state auditors may also expect or require GAAP financials as well, so dispensaries will be well advised to produce GAAP financial statements whether or not required for compliance.

Financial Statements

The primary financial reports for the purposes of a cannabis business that is not publicly traded (on a stock exchange) are the Balance Sheet, Income Statement, and Statement of Cash Flows:

- A cannabis company wants to produce a balance sheet because many of the expenses captured here can be allocated to COGS to lower taxes. The Balance Sheet shows a company's financial position and is essentially a snapshot at the end of the reporting period. The businesses assets, liabilities and shareholders' equity are broken down into their individual components, such as fixed assets (i.e. greenhouse) and long-term liabilities (loans that are to be repaid over the period of greater than one year).

- "Income Statement" is interchangeable with "Profit and Loss," and ultimately shows your net income over the accounting period. Net income is your profit, calculated as sales less COGS, selling, general and administrative expenses, operating expenses, depreciation, interest, taxes and other expenses. You will see your allocations to COGS and how they affect your profit margins on this statement.

- The Statement of Cash Flows is just that, a statement that shows how cash flowed in and out of the business, including the activities it originated from or was spent on. You will want your cannabis CPA/ CFO to project forward cash flows as well to ensure you will have enough green (not the plant) on hand to pay the bills and investors as liabilities come due.

CPA – Certified Public Accountant

It essentially takes a specific route to a master's degree or equivalent, a brutal series of four exams, and some experience to become a CPA. We must comply with ethics and continuing education requirements per our state board of accountancy along with a huge set of standards provided by the AICPA.

CFO – Chief Financial Officer

The executive who directs all financial aspects of a business, including accounting functions, record keeping, designing accounting systems and procedures, financial forecasting, use of funds, etc.

What does "§", "IRC" and "Treasury Regulation" mean?

The "§" is just a symbol to replace the word "section," as in section of the tax code or regulation. The Internal Revenue Service (IRS) is a division of the U.S. Department of the Treasury, so you can surmise that Treasury Regulations are simply the IRS's interpretation of the Internal Revenue Code (IRC). The IRC is the tax code – tax laws as enacted by the United States Congress. You will be able to identify Treasury Regulations as they start with a number one and a period before the number of the tax code section that they are derived from. For example, § 1.471-1 is the Treasury Regulation (*the law*) derived from IRC § 471 (*from the tax code*). As you will see, there are several important Treasury Regulations which arose from Internal Revenue Code § 471 – General rule for inventories. Got it? With no "1." before the number, you're looking at the tax law that Congress came up with, a "1." prefix simply means it's the IRS's rule on the tax law. It's the IRS's job to interpret the law, which is why we should all feel bad for them after the 2018 "Tax Reform."

CHAPTER 7 – INTERNAL CONTROLS

The concept of *internal controls* deserves its own chapter. Auditors will literally ask you for your internal controls procedures, and we don't want that to be the first time you hear the term. Internal controls are essentially the written processes and procedures that you and your employees will be required to follow to show that you have control over your business. Not only will a robust system of internal controls keep you from being robbed (a.k.a. embezzled), but it will establish credibility with state and federal auditors. In our industry, we need to have controls related to the buying, handling and management of inventory from intake to the floor, receiving product, retaining of receipts and manifests, scanning of documents (preferably to the cloud), storage and preparation of cannabis products, security of products, security of cash, security of the facility, expense management, reimbursements, daily cash count, payroll, management of contractors, reconciling accounts, and an entire laundry list of accounting processes. You will need to have a system in place to ensure regulatory reports are made, tax filings are done, 1099s are issued, IDs are copied to records, etc.

Working with your accountants, you will want to establish written internal controls procedures that are strictly enforced. These controls should set the overall tone of the organization. They determine who has authority, who is responsible and accountable for what, and the consequences of failing to adhere to them. Some duties are segregated to minimize the potential for a breakdown in any aspect of control. In a larger organization, internal controls originate with human resources policies and practices related to recruitment, orientation, training, evaluating, counseling, promoting, compensating, and remedial activities. Routine training and regular staff meetings should reinforce expectations – these sessions should be documented and should communicate standards mandated by SOPs (Standard Operating Procedures) and company policies.

Managers of a cannabis business should routinely identify risks. Risks are typically the result of changes, such as new personnel, changes in regulatory or operating environment (laws), new or updated information systems (seed to sale, POS), rapid expansion of operations, new business models, products or activities, corporate restructuring, expansion or acquisition, and changes in procedures (SOPs or Accounting). In addition, anything that could affect your financial statements should be assessed, such as the ability to initiate, authorize, record, process, and report financial data. Once you identify risks, you will be burdened with considering the costs and ramifications of either accepting the risk or working to eliminate it.

Auditors are interested in your accounting information processes as they pertain to financial reporting. They should be able to track items from the initiation of a transaction to the inclusion in your financial statements, and see that appropriate disclosures are made in those financial statements. In cannabis, this will include how you make estimates or track items that are allocated to your Cost of Goods Sold. Your accounting system should capture all significant events, accounting records, supporting information and should identify the parties involved in initiating, authorizing, recording, processing, and reporting transactions.

Management is responsible for developing, monitoring and evaluating the control activities and should establish an internal audit function to identify strengths and weaknesses as well as areas for improvement. Some routine control activities include the prenumbering of documents to assure that all transactions are recorded, and no transactions are recorded more than once, authorization of certain transactions, independent checks made to maintain asset accountability including verification of work by others (i.e., review of bank reconciliations, comparison of subsidiary records to control accounts, and comparison of physical counts of inventory to perpetual records). Documentation should be maintained to provide evidence of transactions to be recorded. Performance reviews should compare actual performance to budgets, forecasts, and prior periods, and compare financial and non-financial information (i.e., evaluating cannabis prices vs. customer activity).

Safeguarding assets is a necessity in the cannabis industry, and physical controls are a means to achieve this. Physical segregation and security of assets can be accomplished with safes or protective devices. Consider authorizing access to assets and records (such as through computer access codes, prenumbered forms, and required signatures on documents for the removal or disposition of assets), and periodic counting and comparison of actual assets with amounts shown in accounting records. One example would be having door locks re-keyed quarterly or when an employee with a key is terminated for any reason. In cannabis, we suggest a daily check that no secured area or secured storage or vault is unlocked and that security cameras are operational, for example.

Segregation of duties ensures that individuals do not perform incompatible duties. Duties should be segregated so that the work of one individual provides a crosscheck on another's work. Assigning different people to the responsibilities of authorizing transactions, recording transactions, and maintaining custody of the related assets reduces the opportunities for any individual to both perpetrate and conceal errors or fraud in the normal course of duties. An example is to have one employee review POS systems and cross-check with another employee to cash received. Similarly, one employee may verify the weight of product on hand at the end of the day while another cross-checks the seed to sale tracking system.

Internal controls not only prevent fraud but show investors and auditors that you are running a tight ship. Even if you are a very small operation, you will want to possess and adhere to a solid set of internal controls.

Part IV: Cannabis Taxation and Rules for Inventories

(OR § 280E AND § 471)

CHAPTER 8 – THE INFAMOUS § 280E

"No deduction or credit shall be allowed for any amount paid or incurred during the taxable year in carrying on any trade or business if such trade or business (or the activities which comprise such trade or business) consists of trafficking in controlled substances (within the meaning of schedule I and II of the Controlled Substances Act) which is prohibited by Federal law or the law of any State in which such trade or business is conducted."

– Congress in 1982

The quote above is the <u>entire</u> **26 U.S. Code § 280E – Expenditures in connection with the illegal sale of drugs**. That single sentence turns the tax treatment of cannabis touching businesses upside-down and makes the required accounting an overly complex set of never-ending tasks. It complicates general business decisions, such as entity selection and building layout, rendering status quo advice from non-cannabis professionals useless or incorrect in many instances. We will tell you why § 280E arose, how it hurts your state legal cannabis business, and what you can do about it. This chapter is a great place to start for the practitioner considering servicing the industry but is intended for a Cannabis CEO dedicated to being on top of his/ her game.

§ 280E is Congress's way of punishing illegal drug dealers. As you will see below, Jeff Edmondson used laws existing in the 1970's to beat the IRS in U.S. Tax Court and was able receive the same tax deductions as any legal business could *at the time.* The thing is, he was peddling methamphetamine, cocaine and marijuana back when there was no law in place to prevent him from claiming deductions for typical business expenses. In 1982 Congress implemented § 280E to prevent drug dealers from taking tax deductions for otherwise "normal" business expenses related to the trafficking of illegal drugs.

Drilling down a bit further, if you sell any drugs that are classified as schedule I or II under the Controlled Substances Act of 1970, you are not entitled to the tax write-offs that nearly all other businesses are allowed for ordinary and necessary business expenses. Cannabis is currently Schedule I, so despite being legal under most state's laws, it is still illegal at the federal level. Federal laws trump state laws, so state legal cannabis touching businesses are not treated the same a federally legal business. It is important to note that it is possible to have separate lines of business that are non-cannabis touching in concert with your cannabis business, but this is not as simple as it sounds. We will discuss in Chapter 7 along with the pertinent court case, *CHAMP v. Commissioner (of the IRS).*

The only saving grace is the good old Constitution of the United States of America, which limited Congress's power to stripping a cannabis business of its deduction but does **not** allow the taxation of the return of capital to the business, which we know as a cannabis business's Cost of Goods Sold (COGS). You can only be taxed on income, and since income is your gross receipts (a.k.a. revenue) less the cost of the goods you sell, you effectively get a deduction for the costs that can be allocated to your cannabis products if you follow the tax laws and regulations that apply to inventories (more on § 471 later). These complex rules require that specific methods of accounting be done on a continuing basis. If these regulations are not properly adhered to, the results will be the overpayment of taxes or worse – penalties, fines, noncompliance with state laws, unanticipated tax liabilities, and possibly being shut down. This chapter and chapter 16 will shed light on how these unfortunate circumstances may arise.

We will also discuss some tactics for ensuring you get the COGS you are entitled to, thereby minimizing the taxes paid under § 280E. Separate lines of business, the physical layout of your operation, cost accounting and issuing Generally Accepted Accounting Principles (GAAP) financial statements are addressed.

Caution: drug traffickers, state legal or not, are absolutely required to file a federal tax return! Failure to file has landed canna-business owners in the can, as you will see in the chapter 16.

Why § 280E Punishes Your Cannabis Business

Question: Who in the hell is Jeffrey Edmondson?
Answer: The guy we can blame for the punitive tax law, § 280E.

In 1974, when Mr. Edmondson was convicted of selling large quantities of meth pills, cocaine and weed, the IRS immediately attempted to collect about $17,000 in back taxes from him. Jeff smartly filed a tax return in 1975, and relying on the "Cohan rule," which allows approximations in the reasonable absence of records (because who would maintain records of illegal drug deals?), Edmondson's testimony of his expenses for the illicit drug business was taken into consideration by the Tax Court. Would you believe that Jeff was allowed deductions for many of the expenses that he incurred in the normal line of business (drug dealing), including over $100,000 in costs for the actual narcotics. The court wrote,

> "The nature of petitioner's role in the drug market, together with his appearance and candor at trial, cause us to believe that he was honest, forthright, and candid in his reconstruction of the income and expenses from his illegal activities in the taxable year 1974."

A 1981 Tax Court Memorandum held that Edmondson's "cost of goods sold for the taxable year 1974 was $105,300," and allowed him tax deductions such as one-third of the rent paid for his apartment (drug storage), costs of paraphernalia, mileage, etc. Edmondson even wrote off the cost of the scale that he weighed his drugs on, as well as bills for the rotary telephone he used to set up drug deals. At the time, a drug trafficking business was treated just as any other trade or business for tax purposes and allowed deductions for ordinary and necessary expenses under IRC § 162(a).

You can imagine that the "just say no to drugs" folks were not happy. Enter a pissed off 97th Congress, who enacted Internal Revenue Code § 280E in the Tax Equity and Fiscal Responsibility Act of 1982:

> "No deduction or credit shall be allowed for any amount paid or incurred during the taxable year in carrying on any trade or business if such trade or business (or the activities which comprise such trade or business) consists of trafficking in controlled substances (within the meaning of schedule I and II of the Controlled Substances Act) which is prohibited by Federal law or the law of any State in which such trade or business is conducted."

Congress enacted § 280E, the bane of your existence, thanks to the "honest, forthright, and candid" Jeffrey Edmondson. Great guy if you're the one collecting taxes. § 280E makes accounting complex if you want to remain IRS compliant and get deductions for the Cost of Goods Sold, but also results in the exclusion from deductibility of items that cannot be allocated to the Cost of Goods Sold, such as marketing and general selling and administrative expenses.

Thanks a lot Jeff – making the simple difficult since September 3rd, 1982!

How § 280E Punishes Your Cannabis Business

If you want to get technical, legal and illegal businesses are required to pay taxes on gross income per IRC § 61(a). The difference for a cannabis business is that § 280E disallows all deductions (a.k.a. write-offs) that almost all other business take advantage of to lower their taxable income. Since § 280E is specific to those trafficking in Schedule I or II drugs, cannabis touching businesses can't utilize tax write-offs including phone, auto, rents, utilities, employee wages, etc., but can allocate some or portions of some of these expenses to COGS.

Deductions are determined by the "legislative grace" of Congress; however, the Costs of Goods Sold are excepted from the disallowance created by § 280E, as taxing beyond income is unconstitutional. Specifically, the 16th Amendment of the Constitution allows Congress the power to "...collect tax on incomes, from whatever source derived...." Tax law provides us with a definition of "gross income" being equal to "the total sales, less the cost of goods sold."

Essentially, Congress can tax income derived from capital but cannot tax the return (to you) of the capital itself. This means you can recover your investment in your cannabis products once they are sold. Think of capital as the financial assets or financial value of assets used in business operations to buy or manufacture products or provide services. Capital and COGS are somewhat synonymous for our purposes. Since COGS lowers the amount of income that is taxable, it has the same effect as a tax deduction. Although we may use the phrase, "Cost of Goods Sold deduction," technically, COGS is not a deduction but an adjustment to gross receipts to arrive at gross income. Thankfully, as you will see later in the chapter, the excise taxes levied on cannabis are another downward adjustment to gross receipts (otherwise you would be taxed twice).

Many cannabis entrepreneurs are aware that deductions aren't allowed in their cannabis business but might overlook the disallowance of tax credits in the language, "No deduction or credit shall be allowed...." We underlined "credit" as we thought we should remind you in case you were looking for that $7,500 tax credit for your MMJ delivery service Tesla.

Is § 280E Forever?

To date, some have unsuccessfully brought the IRS to task in Tax Court, claiming that the onerous § 280E was never intended to apply to medical marijuana. The IRS is getting a bad rap from cannabis entrepreneurs for § 280E; however, they will be the first to point out that only an act of Congress can repeal or amend §

280E to exclude medical and/ or recreational marijuana. Alternatively, the DEA holds another possible key to the cannabis industry circumventing § 280E: modifying the scheduling of cannabis under the Controlled Substances Act. § 280E does not apply to Schedule III, IV, or V drugs. As long as THC containing products are Schedule I (currently) or II, you will have to jump through hoops for COGS deductions.

§ 280E in Action

Let's run through a hypothetical example which is displayed in Table 2 below. On the left we have "Joe's Used Tires," a typical business that sells old tires. In the middle, we have a dispensary, "COGSLESS Canna" who doesn't keep records or account for their COGS. On the right, we have "Black Tie Edibles." owned and operated by a retired pastry chef (Bob) and his investor buddy, Mr. Suit.

Similarities Among All Three Businesses

All three businesses are taxed as C Corporations and have the same $5 million in revenues. All three businesses spent $2.5 million on expenses allocable to the cost of the goods they sold, so they all have the same gross income. All three spent another $1.5 million on what would be deductible business expenses for a normal business, but as we know, Congress disallows deductions for these ordinary and necessary business expenses via § 280E.

Joes Used Tires

Joe sold $5 million worth of tires and tire-related products and services. He spent $2.5 million on the goods he sold and another $1.5 million on ordinary and necessary business expenses for a total of $4 million. His net income is his taxable income in this simplified scenario, so he pays 21% in federal taxes as a corporation and is left with $790,000.

COGSLESS Canna

These guys grow the best bud in the Emerald Triangle, but they just didn't have the time to keep track of their books and records in their first full year of operations. All they know is that they had $1 million in cash at year end after they sold about $5 million worth of flower in their vertically integrated cultivation/

dispensary business. In theory*, since they didn't keep any records of expenses, let alone tie them to the COGS, they get no tax deductions at all due to § 280E. They would pay 21% on their total sales, or $1,050,000 in federal income tax, leaving them with a net loss of $50,000 on the year. They violated the old Wall Street rule of never letting a profit turn into a loss.

*We say, "in theory." because an IRS audit may allow for some COGS after the fact based on industry ratios or other factors beyond the scope of this book; however, this is not a process you want to go through.

Black Tie Edibles

Mr. Suit has invested in several other cannabis businesses, so he brought his Cannabis CPA onboard when he and Chef Bob decided to go into the edibles business. They know that a cannabis business is taxed on gross income and not allowed any "normal" business expenses, so they hired an expert to allocate as many expenses as possible to COGS, so they won't be taxed on that amount. Their CPA was able to allocate $2.5 million to COGS during the year. The other $1.5 million of normal business expenses were subjected to § 280E and disallowed as a deduction, but they were still well in the green after paying a 21% corporate tax rate on the $2.5 million of sales not attributed to COGS.

Corporations> Subject to flat 21% Corporate Tax Rate	*Joes Used Tires* Typical-Biz	*COGSLESS Canna* Canna-Biz w/out COGS Dedcution	*Black Tie Edibles* Canna-Biz w/ Proper Accounting
Sales	$ 5,000,000	$ 5,000,000	$ 5,000,000
COGS	$ (2,500,000)	$ (2,500,000)	$ (2,500,000)
Gross Income	$ 2,500,000	$ 2,500,000	$ 2,500,000
Business Expenses	$ (1,500,000)	$ (1,500,000)	$ (1,500,000)
280E Disallowed		$ 4,000,000	$ 1,500,000
Taxable Income	$ 1,000,000	$ 5,000,000	$ 2,500,000
Net Income	$ 1,000,000	$ 1,000,000	$ 1,000,000
Federal Tax 21%	$ (210,000)	$ (1,050,000)	$ (525,000)
Net Profit or (Loss)	$ 790,000	$ (50,000)	$ 475,000

Table 2: Example of Proper Cannabis Accounting

Conclusion

All things being equal, the simple application of § 280E discriminately turns a $790,000 profit for Joes Used Tires into a $475,000 profit for Black Tie Edibles. In a high margin industry, as cannabis has been, there is still room to turn a profit even after the punitive tax law is applied; however, the failure of COGSLESS Canna to seek some form of § 280E relief through proper cannabis accounting could sink an otherwise profitable business before it is afloat.

CHAPTER 9 – MINIMIZING THE IMPACT OF § 280E

The two Tax Court cases in this chapter demonstrate the opposite end of the spectrum when it comes to setting up a second line of business that is not subject to § 280E. The facts and circumstances surrounding any second line of business will differ, but these cases are a good starting point as to what may or may not be acceptable to the IRS. Also, without good record keeping and proper cannabis accounting, any argument before the Tax Court is moot.

Separate Line of Non-§ 280E Business?

(CHAMP & Olive Court Cases)

It is possible to have a separate line of business by performing activities outside of § 280E in parallel with your cannabis business; however, there must be a mountain of evidence to satisfy the IRS that it is indeed a separate, distinct line of business based upon the economic interrelationship between the lines of business.

In a battle with the IRS, Californians Helping to Alleviate Medical Problems (CHAMP) satisfied the 9th Circuit Court that although they were a dispensary, medical marijuana was just one of the many services they provided. They convinced the court that they also had a distinct palliative care business (*palliative* means specializing in compassionate medical care for people with serious illnesses). The IRS initially disallowed their deductions for the caregiving line of business under the auspices of § 280E. The Court put the second line of business to the tests of the tax rules, particularly, Treas. Reg. § 1.183-2(b). To be a line of business that performs an activity with a profit motive, the Court weighs nine factors (and each factor can have a different weight depending upon its relevance). Those factors are:

1. The manner in which the taxpayer carried on the activity,
2. The expertise of the taxpayer or his or her advisers,
3. The time and effort expended by the taxpayer in carrying on the activity,
4. The expectation that the assets used in the activity may appreciate in value,
5. The success of the taxpayer in carrying on other similar or dissimilar activities,
6. The taxpayer's history of income or loss with respect to the activity,
7. The amount of occasional profits, if any, which are earned,
8. The financial status of the taxpayer, and
9. Elements of personal pleasure or recreation.

CHAMP is a not-for profit-clinic for folks with AIDS, cancer, and M.S. that provides medical marijuana. The caregiving portion of the business charged a monthly fee for counseling and other health-related services. CHAMP had physicians on staff as well. The tax court recognized that they had a very specific, deeply involved and continuing line of business aside from dispensing marijuana. The Tax Court decided in favor of CHAMP and, in summary, said that they operated two distinct trades or businesses and allocated their income to § 280E and non-§ 280E.

CHAMP provided a high burden of evidence that they were not only a dispensary. If you are doing something like this, you want to be working in the health care community, have informational brochures, a library, physicians on staff, labeling to show the type of effect that a strain of marijuana is meant to treat, counseling, etc. You will also want to have membership agreements in place that are to provide services other than marijuana dispensing. Simply selling tee-shirts and glass is not going to cut it.

By establishing a second line of business, CHAMP now increased their profit and loss statement from two categories (§ 280E and COGS) to four. They had § 280E and COGS on the marijuana dispensary side, normal business expenses for palliative care on the other side, and costs that could be allocated between the two (such as the scenario discussed in chapter 2, where a supervisor's salary was divided between § 280E and non-§ 280E).

In contrast to CHAMP, in *Olive vs. Commissioner (of the IRS)* the court held that the owner of a medical marijuana dispensary was not entitled to any business tax deductions, including expenses associated with caregiving services as his business consisted solely of trafficking marijuana and was thereby subject to § 280E. Martin Olive, the owner of the *Vapor Room* in San Francisco, attempted to rely on the CHAMP case to show that he had a separate line of business. First off, the name *Vapor Room* implies smoke, and nothing but smoke. The Vapor Room provided free perks to marijuana dispensary customers, including yoga classes, and movies.

Initially, the IRS said that the Vapor Room's business expenses were unsubstantiated due to poor record keeping. To make a long story short, the Tax Court determined that the sale of medical marijuana in the Vapor Room was inseparable from the other services and perks that they provided. The only significant form of income generation for the business was the sale of marijuana. The Court used an analogy to justify its decision, comparing one bookstore that sells books and provides food for free with another bookstore that sells books and has a café area selling food. The court noted that while the first bookstore would be in the "trade or business" of selling only books, while the other would have two different "trade[s] or business[es]": one sells books and the other food.

On the heels of *Olive v. Commissioner*, a Tax Court Memorandum citing this case was issued in *Canna Care, Inc. v. Commissioner*, stating that, "Aside from the sale of medical marijuana, petitioner's only other source of income was the sale of books, T-shirts, and other items." Canna Care, Inc. was similarly denied their attempt of having a second line of business not subject to § 280E.

When establishing a separate line of business, consider these cases. The deciding factor is substance over form. Remember, this is art more than science and conclusions are determined on a case by case basis. Consider that in Colorado, state law requires that there can only be one customer in the dispensary per Budtender. Because of this, it is common to have a waiting area that does not dispense or contain marijuana products. If you were to sell glass or tee-shirts in this area and had a separate point-of-sale system and a designated cashier, the IRS may take into consideration that law requires this setup and therefore it is a non-§ 280E line of business (we don't know what they would do in each scenario, although we have heard that this worked in an IRS audit). If this were another state that did not require the one Budtender per customer rule, this may or may not work. The Olive and CHAMP cases only reinforce the complexity of operating under § 280E.

What can be done to minimize the impacts of § 280E?

A cannabis business can legally reduce taxes by allocating expenses to the Cost of Goods Sold (COGS). To ensure dispensaries, grows, extractors, edible manufacturers, etc. are not taxed on the cost of these goods, they must do proper accrual/ cost accounting. To absolutely minimize the tax that you pay as a cannabis touching business, manufacturers/ producers must do recurring cost accounting in accordance with GAAP (Generally Accepted Accounting Principles). Internal Revenue Code § 471 allows the capitalization of the costs that go into your marijuana product inventory, essentially allowing a tax deduction for the costs traceable to that inventory upon its sale.

Thus, any cost properly included in inventory may be capitalized to inventory and deducted, but only if COGS is computed per the appropriate tax rules. The line between COGS and the disallowed deductions of § 280E is drawn by the inventory capitalization rules that define the cost of inventory, and thereby the COGS.

COGS Calculation

Below is a rudimentary example of how Cost of Goods Sold is calculated. Using Black Tie Edibles from our example above, let's say they had $100,000 in finished goods (edible candies) sitting in their safe at midnight on 12/31/2017. During the year, they were able to allocate $2.9 million to COGS. Added together, they had a total of $3 million worth of inventory available for sale throughout the year and ended 2018 with $600,000 worth of goods in the safe, $450,000 of which was ready to ship in the first week of 2019, and the other $150,000 of which was 100 pounds of cannabis flower for the next batch. Doing the math, you would see that they sold $2,500,000 worth of goods in 2018. Remember, the "COGS deduction" can only be taken upon sale of the goods, so the $450,000 sitting in the safe until 2019 is not yet COGS.

Inventory at Start of Year 1/1/2018	$	100,000
Plus: Inventory Costs Incurred in Year	$	2,900,000
Cost of Goods Available for Sale	$	3,000,000
Less: Ending Inventory 12/31/2018	$	(600,000)
COGS	$	2,500,000

CHAPTER 10 – ACCOUNTING FOR INVENTORIES (§ 471)

All you really need to know about § 471 is that the regulations derived from it are *the* playbook that dictates which expenses we can or cannot allocate to cannabis inventory. We want to allocate as much as legally possible so that we can deduct the expenses tied to Cost of Goods Sold (COGS) as sales are made. This chapter will break down which rules derived from § 471 apply to cultivators, growers, manufacturers, extractors, etc., or retailers (dispensaries). We'll quote some of the relevant tax laws and regulations and summarize what specifically you can deduct and under which circumstances. We'll do a "translation" of some of these complex rules, so you know what it means for your business.

To be compliant with the IRS and to maximize your tax write-offs you need to follow IRC § 471's regulations regarding inventory. Many state cannabis laws specifically require Generally Accepted Accounting Principles (GAAP) cost accounting as well, entailing adherence to these tax regulations.

To recap, we want to minimize the amount of income subject to federal tax under the punitive tax law, § 280E, so we must correctly calculate your COGS. COGS is not subject to income tax, but we must consistently and properly allocate costs per regulations § 1.471-11 or -3 to cannabis products which are specifically identified in periodic inventory procedures. Upon sale of these cannabis products, you are allowed your COGS tax deduction.

IRC § 471 – General rule for inventories allows the IRS to prescribe that inventories must be taken so that a taxpayer is using a method of accounting that most clearly reflects income. In the case of cannabis touching businesses, this would be accomplished by capitalizing COGS into inventory per Treasury Regulation §1.471-3 or -11. If inventories are required, then the accrual method of accounting must be used as it pertains to purchases and sales unless the IRS explicitly permits a cash or modified cash method of accounting (unusual and undesirable).

TRANSLATION: In most cases, a cannabis touching company will be required by the IRS to take inventory on a recurring basis and to use the prescribed inventory/ accrual method of accounting (vs. cash basis or modified cash basis).

Capitalization

You will need to know what "capitalization" means to understand why these § 471 rules are important. It's not terribly difficult: just picture an ounce of marijuana that resulted from a grow operation. If the inventory rules of § 471 allow $80 of expenses to be allocated to that ounce of inventory, you are capitalizing $80 into that ounce. Only when you sell that ounce are you allowed the $80 deduction for COGS. In the meantime, the $80 potential deduction is capitalized to the inventory, or "stuck" there for a lack of a better explanation. It doesn't matter if you sell it for $100 or $200; COGS is $80. Clearly you want to capitalize as many expenses as are reasonable into the cost of your inventory. This is another example where a "normal business" would want to do the opposite. In a non-cannabis business, you would want to take expenses as a deduction immediately and not capitalize them if not required to. Unfortunately, § 280E eliminates this option for cannabis touching businesses.

Capitalization is otherwise defined as deferring the recognition of an expense by treating the item as a fixed asset rather than recognizing the cost in the period that it was incurred. How, and how often this is required to be done is the debate among CPA's allocating costs to inventory under IRC § 471. Must it be done monthly, quarterly or annually? We prescribe quarterly or monthly depending upon your business's circumstances if GAAP financials are required to maximize tax deductions. For resellers (dispensaries), we suggest quarterly and GAAP financials; however, annual allocations are acceptable if GAAP financials are not being issued.

§ 1.471-1 Need for inventories.

This regulation (in its entirety below) tells you what to include in inventory:

> "In order to reflect taxable income correctly, inventories at the beginning and end of each taxable year are necessary in every case in which the production, purchase, or sale of merchandise is an income-producing factor. The inventory should include all finished or partly finished goods and, in the case of raw materials and supplies, only those which have been acquired for sale or which will physically become a part of merchandise intended for sale, in which class fall containers, such as kegs, bottles, and cases, whether returnable or not, if title thereto will pass to the purchaser of the product to be sold therein. Merchandise should be included in the inventory only if title thereto is vested in the taxpayer. Accordingly, the seller should include in his inventory goods under contract for sale but not yet segregated and applied to the contract and goods out upon consignment but should exclude from inventory goods sold (including containers), title to which has passed to the purchaser. A purchaser should include in inventory merchandise purchased (including containers), title to which has passed to him, although such merchandise is in transit or for other reasons has not been reduced to physical possession, but should not include goods ordered for future delivery, transfer of title to which has not yet been effected. (But see § 1.472-1.)"

TRANSLATION: Your cannabis company will have inventory in various forms (finished cannabis goods, work in process, raw materials and supplies) at the beginning and end of each tax year. Remember, you only get your deduction in the year in which the finished goods are sold.

§ 1.471-3(b) Inventories at cost – Dispensaries (Retailers)

"In the case of merchandise purchased since the beginning of the taxable year, the invoice price less trade or other discounts, except strictly cash discounts approximating a fair interest rate, which may be deducted or not at the option of the taxpayer, provided a consistent course is followed. To this net invoice price should be added transportation or other necessary charges incurred in acquiring possession of the goods. For taxpayers acquiring merchandise for resale that are subject to the provisions of section 263A, see §§ 1.263A-1 and 1.263A-3 for additional amounts that must be included in inventory costs."

NOTE: Don't look to § 263A until you see more on it at the end of this chapter.

TRANSLATION: Dispensaries can deduct the net expense of the cannabis products they buy for resale, plus the cost of transportation, repackaging (labeling or making pre-rolled joints, etc.), and some of the overhead associated with maintaining inventory and storing the cannabis products.

Cultivation/ Manufacturer – Applicable Regulations:

§ 1.471-3(c) of **Inventories at cost** and

§ 1. 471-11 **Inventories of manufacturers**

§ 1.471-3(c) " In the case of merchandise produced by the taxpayer since the beginning of the taxable year, (1) the cost of raw materials and supplies entering into or consumed in connection with the product, (2) expenditures for direct labor, and (3) indirect production costs incident to and necessary for the production of the particular article, including in such indirect production costs an appropriate portion of management expenses, but not including any cost of selling or return on capital, whether by way of interest or profit. See §§ 1.263A-1 and 1.263A-2 for more specific rules regarding the treatment of production costs."

TRANSLATION: The costs that can be tied to producing your cannabis products can be allocated to inventory; selling expenses (a.k.a. trafficking) and profits cannot.

Full Absorption Method of Inventory Costing

§ 1.471-11 is quite lengthy. We won't kill trees on the entire text, but we will summarize it and include some excerpts. If you are required to change to this method of accounting, you will have to elect it via IRS Form 3115.

§ 1.471-11(a) requires the "full absorption method of inventory costing," which means you must allocate the direct and indirect costs of production to your inventory in the tax year it is produced, whether sold during that year or not. The definition of "financial reports" is included here, "financial reports (including consolidated financial statements) to shareholders, partners, beneficiaries or other proprietors and for credit purposes."

§ 1.471-11(b) spells out that "direct production costs" and "indirect production costs" are those costs incident to and necessary for production or manufacturing operations. This part explains what these items are.

§ 1.471-11(c) tells you what you must include in inventory, what you can include if you take specified actions, and what you cannot include in inventory.

Here is what you **MUST INCLUDE** in inventory if you are a cultivator/ producer/ manufacturer:

> § 1.471-11(c)(2) Includability of certain indirect production costs -
> (i)Indirect production costs included in inventoriable costs. Indirect production costs which must enter into the computation of the amount of inventoriable costs (regardless of their treatment by a taxpayer in his financial reports) include:
> (a) Repair expenses,
> (b) Maintenance,
> (c) Utilities, such as heat, power and light,
> (d) Rent,
> (e) Indirect labor and production supervisory wages, including basic compensation, overtime pay, vacation and holiday pay, sick leave pay (other than payments pursuant to a wage continuation plan under section 105(d), shift differential, payroll taxes and contributions to a supplemental unemployment benefit plan,
> (f) Indirect materials and supplies,
> (g) Tools and equipment not capitalized, and

(h) Costs of quality control and inspection,
to the extent, and only to the extent, such costs are incident to and necessary for production or manufacturing operations or processes.

Here is what you **CANNOT INCLUDE** in inventory if you are a cultivator/ producer/ manufacturer:

§ 1.471-11(c) (ii)Costs not included in inventoriable costs. Costs which are not required to be included for tax purposes in the computation of the amount of inventoriable costs (regardless of their treatment by a taxpayer in his financial reports) include:
(a) Marketing expenses,
(b) Advertising expenses,
(c) Selling expenses,
(d) Other distribution expenses,
(e) Interest,
(f) Research and experimental expenses including engineering and product development expenses,
(g) Losses under section 165 and the regulations thereunder,
(h) Percentage depletion in excess of cost depletion,
(i) Depreciation and amortization reported for Federal income tax purposes in excess of depreciation reported by the taxpayer in his financial reports,
(j) Income taxes attributable to income received on the sale of inventory,
(k) Pension contributions to the extent that they represent past services cost,
(l) General and administrative expenses incident to and necessary for the taxpayer's activities as a whole rather than to production or manufacturing operations or processes, and
(m) Salaries paid to officers attributable to the performance of services which are incident to and necessary for the taxpayer's activities taken as a whole rather than to production or manufacturing operations or processes.

Here is what you **CAN** include in inventory ONLY IF you consistently include these items in **GAAP FINANCIAL STATEMENTS**:

By issuing financial statements in accordance with GAAP (Generally Accepted Accounting Principles), additional expenses may be allocated under regulation § 1.471-11(c)(2)(iii) to maximize COGS, resulting in the absolute minimum in taxes levied under IRC § 280E.

> § 1.471-11(c) (iii) ...The costs listed in this subdivision are:
> (a) Taxes. Taxes otherwise allowable as a deduction under section 164 (other than State and local and foreign income taxes) attributable to assets incident to and necessary for production or manufacturing operations or processes. Thus, for example, the cost of State and local property taxes imposed on a factory or other production facility and any State and local taxes imposed on inventory must be included in or excluded from the computation of the amount of inventoriable costs for tax purposes depending upon their treatment by a taxpayer in his financial reports.
> (b) Depreciation and depletion. Depreciation reported in financial reports and cost depletion on assets incident to and necessary for production or manufacturing operations or processes. In computing cost depletion under this section, the adjusted basis of such assets shall be reduced by cost depletion and not by percentage depletion taken thereon.
> (c) Employee benefits. Pension and profit-sharing contributions representing current service costs otherwise allowable as a deduction under section 404, and other employee benefits incurred on behalf of labor incident to and necessary for production or manufacturing operations or processes. These other benefits include workmen's compensation expenses, payments under a wage continuation plan described in section 105(d), amounts of a type which would be includible in the gross income of employees under non-qualified pension, profit-sharing and stock bonus plans, premiums on life and health insurance and miscellaneous benefits provided for employees such as safety, medical treatment, cafeteria, recreational facilities, membership dues, etc., which are otherwise allowable as deductions under chapter 1 of the Code.
> (d) Costs attributable to strikes, rework labor, scrap and spoilage. Costs attributable to rework labor, scrap and spoilage which are incident to and necessary for

production or manufacturing operations or processes and costs attributable to strikes incident to production or manufacturing operation or processes.
(e) Factory administrative expenses. Administrative costs of production (but not including any cost of selling or any return on capital) incident to and necessary for production or manufacturing operations or processes.
(f) Officers' salaries. Salaries paid to officers attributable to services performed incident to and necessary for production or manufacturing operations or processes.
(g) Insurance costs. Insurance costs incident to and necessary for production or manufacturing operations or processes such as insurance on production machinery and equipment.

Note that costs similar to those mentioned in § 1.471-11(c)(i) and (ii) may be included in the appropriate category, and anything that isn't similar is specified in part (iii).

TRANSLATION: Here is what your cannabis business may be able to deduct:

What Might You be Able to Deduct?

Costs of Goods Sold with proper inventory/ accrual/ cost accounting include:

Direct Costs

- The cannabis crop: seeds, plants, clones, pesticides, nutrients, water, grow/ cleaning supplies, fertilizer, packaging, printing and design, testing and lab fees, pH testers, paraphernalia, etc.
- Retail items: Invoice price of cannabis purchased, less trade or other discounts and transportation or other necessary charges incurred in acquiring inventory of cannabis for resale
- Labor directly involved with purchasing, handling, planting, cultivating, harvesting, trimming, etc.
    - o Associated workers' comp, payroll taxes, holiday and vacation pay, OT, and fringe benefits such as life, health and dental insurance
- Subcontractors and temporary labor related to production with or without a 1099 issued

- Some management company costs have been allocated but may not be recommended for dispensaries and cultivation operations

Indirect Costs

- Utilities such as water and electricity/ fuel and security systems – all used in the cultivation facility
- Rent for cultivation facility, storage/warehousing space (possibly a portion of the dispensary)
- Indirect labor, such as for security guards or cleaning the cultivation facility, etc.
- Repairs, maintenance, cleaning supplies as well as some tools and equipment/ rental equipment
- Quality Control and inspection costs, sampling and R&D
- Licensing of cultivation facilities, vehicles, legal and professional services for cultivation facilities

Additional Costs of Goods Sold when included in GAAP Financial Statements

- State/ local/ foreign real and personal property taxes and general sales tax up to aggregate $10k
- Crop damage/ forced destruction of a crop, costs attributed to strikes, rework, scrap and spoilage
- Depreciation reported in financials for equipment used in manufacturing, extracting, etc.
- Employee benefits to extent related to labor above (401(k) plans, profit sharing, workers' comp, stock bonus plans, life and health ins prem, cafeteria plans, gym memberships, medical treatments, recreational facilities and gym membership dues, etc.)
- Performing inventory and administrative functions related to manufacturing (not cost accounting)
- Officers' salaries that can be traced to the production, extraction, or manufacturing of cannabis or its extracted material
- Most of the insurance costs that are attributable to the production and extraction (both for the facility and the equipment in the facility) of cannabis

Allocation Methods

We can't emphasize enough that when you allocate expenses to non-§ 280E, you want to specifically identify what is not subject to § 280E, not the other way around. For example, you carve out the portion of the dispensary where the non-§ 280E activities occur and document the time, activities, and overhead that are required for this aspect of the business, then determine that anything not documented here is "§ 280E." Do not document what is § 280E and say everything else is COGS – we doubt any auditor will accept this.

If you are wondering how to slice the expenses that are a portion of each § 280E and non-§ 280E, the permissible methods of allocating costs to inventory are described in § 1.471-11(d). You may use the "manufacturing burden rate," the "standard cost method," and the "practical capacity concept." Basically, any consistent and reasonable method of making allocations may be used. We will spare you the details, as they will be applied to your inventory on a case by case basis.

§263A (UNICAP Rules) and Chief Counsel Advice (CCA) 201504011 (UPDATE 12/18)

§263A UNICAP is relevant because by following these rules you would get additional costs into inventory and lower your tax liability, but to make a long story short, on November 29, 2018, in the case of Harborside v. Commissioner, the Judge issued a precedent setting opinion that § 263A does not apply to cannabis. This reiterates the IRS via Chief Counsel Advice 201504011 which guides businesses subject to § 280E to apply the inventory rules per § 471 as it existed in 1982 when § 280E was enacted. Unfortunately, the Uniform Capitalization (or UNICAP) rules of § 263A did not exist at this time (they arrived in 1986).

Harborside v. Commissioner (UPDATE 12/18)

The Harborside v. Commissioner (of the IRS) decision came down on November 29, 2018 as a Tax Court Opinion, meaning it is binding and precedent setting.

This case began in 2010, and the only major revelation is that the IRS's Chief Counsel Advice "CCA 201504011" has merit. § 263A is now clearly NOT an option as a means of capitalizing cannabis inventory. The case also reiterates that lines of business that have a "close and inseparable organizational and economic relationship" will not be treated as two separate businesses for tax purposes. If inseparable - one business cannot live without the other - then all lines of business are treated as one subject to §280E. Many industry participants incorrectly believe that using multiple business entities, particularly management companies, will allow them to skirt §280E.

These 62 pages of the case are worth a read as it is entertaining at points. Judge Holmes is a comedian.

Harborside Health Center, among the largest medical marijuana dispensaries in America, disobeyed the IRS and was thereby disallowed additional Cost of Goods Sold (COGS) "deductions" calculated under the more favorable § 263A UNICAP inventory method. They were penalized by the IRS for not following IRC § 471 as was suggested by CCA 201504011. The IRS CCA (Chief Counsel Advice) was not precedent setting and was considered to be unconstitutional by many in the know, so it is no wonder that the attorney who won the "CHAMPS. v. Commissioner" case, Henry Wykowski (along with attorney Matthew Williams), was champing at the bit (pun intended) to challenge the IRS.

Harborside was a non-profit (this status is recognized under CA state law, but not federally for a cannabis business) and operated as a collective for the years under scrutiny (2007 – 2012), meaning patients were the providers, employees, and consumers of all marijuana. About 99% of Harborside's sales during that period were cannabis: clones, flower, manufactured goods.

Initially, the federal government attempted a forfeiture action against the business for nothing more than being a state legal cannabis company – the government's action was promptly dismissed. IRS audits followed and resulted in the assessment of deficiencies and penalties to the tune of eight figures. $XX,XXX,XXX for emphasis.

The outcome of Harborside's arguments is not surprising – status quo was to be anticipated. Harborside first argued that since the forfeiture action by the government failed, they could not be subjected to § 280E because of a concept called "res judicata," meaning that since the forfeiture action by the government was already settled and they weren't subject to forfeiture, they shouldn't be subject to § 280E either. This effort was futile. Harborside also argued that since Congress could not foresee state legal cannabis when § 280E arose, it should not apply. Once again, a futile effort, as only an act of Congress or the DEA can override § 280E or marijuana's status as Schedule I under the CSA (Controlled Substances Act) respectively.

Harborside tried the separate trade or business route as well (remember, their attorney won CHAMP), but the facts and circumstances surrounding the economic relationship with their other lines of business landed them much closer to Olive v. Commissioner; they lost this argument too.

The real meat of the case, as far as we are concerned, is whether or not the preferable § 263A UNICAP inventory methods could be applied to cannabis businesses. § 263A means cry now, laugh later to a "normal business" (non-cannabis); they are required to include more line items in capitalized indirect costs, but must wait until they realize the related income to take these deductions (this more clearly reflects income, somewhat like GAAP matching principles). Since a "normal business" can immediately deduct the more limited indirect costs allowed by § 471, this method may be more desirable to them because of the time-value-of-money. In cannabis, this is counter-intuitive. Cannabis companies must wait until the sale is made to reduce gross receipts by COGS to arrive at gross income (the 16th Amendment gives Congress the power to tax income only, not the return of capital, a.k.a. COGS). Since a cannabis business must wait until inventory is sold under either § 471 or § 263A if it were allowed, the time value of money is not a consideration, and only the greater latitude to deduct more indirect costs would matter to a cannabis business, creating a tax benefit for cannabis if § 263A was allowed.

That pesky CCA 201504011 recognized this as a "timing issue" when it guided businesses subject to § 280E to apply the inventory rules per § 471 as it existed in 1982 when § 280E was enacted. Unfortunately, the Uniform Capitalization (or UNICAP) rules of § 263A did not exist at this time (they arrived in 1986). Harborside sought to rewrite the definition of COGS by arguing that they were forced to pay more tax than allowed by the Constitution by not being allowed to utilize § 263A. This argument was undoubtedly shot-down as § 263A expressly prohibits capitalizing expenses that would NOT otherwise be deductible. We all know that § 280E says "no deductions."

Harborside also tried to sneak in the idea that they were a "producer" of cannabis in hopes of being allowed the additional COGS of 1.471-11 (as opposed to 1.471-3(b) which applies to resellers). Harborside merely shuffled cannabis clones from wholesalers to their growers and bought back finished product, rendering them a reseller. Strike 5. The only outstanding item from this case is the application of accuracy-related penalties, which will be addressed by the colorful Judge Holmes at another time. Hopefully they are nowhere near eight figures.

A Note on Medical Expense Deductions

Individuals may be allowed medical expense deductions on their 1040 tax return; however, we thought we should point out that the current (2017) revision of IRS Publication 502 states that:

> "You can't include in medical expenses amounts you pay for controlled substances (such as marijuana, laetrile, etc.) that aren't legal under federal law, even if such substances are legalized by state law."

CHAPTER 11 – EXAMPLES OF CANNABIS ACCOUNTING

Grow Operation Example of Allocating COGS

Let's look at a cannabis grow operation:

From the planting of seeds or clones to the sale-ready final product may take 120 – 180 days or so. Stages and activities include vegetation, growing, watering, harvesting, drying, curing, testing at the lab, packaging, labeling the cannabis products and then transporting them to the dispensary. How much does it cost to grow a pound of pot? You start with a seed or a clone which is minimal and is considered "Raw Material." In a cannabis company, your raw materials on hand at the end of an accounting period are usually very low in dollar value. You probably won't have many "Finished Goods" either, because you immediately take your finished products to the dispensary and sell them. This leaves a clear majority of your inventory in the "Work in Progress" (WIP) stage, and the way you value WIP is with a flower calendar. You may have thousands of plants consisting of various strains; for each strain, you need to know how far along it is. You conduct inventory and assign a percentage of completion depending upon how far along you are on your flower calendar. For example, your flower is trimmed and dried and you are picking samples up from lab tomorrow – it is 99% complete.

For each strain, you will need to estimate the yield per strain from your "Operations Farmers Guide" and keep track of how many of each plant you have and how close to complete they are. From there you perform cost accounting and start allocating direct and indirect costs to your crop – items such as direct labor, indirect labor, utilities, security, nutrients, supplies, soil, testing, etc. Keep in mind that if the IRS determines that you are doing this correctly and in accordance with Generally Accepted Accounting Principles (GAAP), you can allocate even more costs; scrap, spoilage, rework, depreciation, etc. to Cost of Goods Sold (COGS) and minimize the taxes you pay. Unfortunately, most cannabis businesses are doing this wrong. Do it right, and you have yourself a competitive advantage.

Ensure your finance/ accounting department is doing it right.

By now you are tired of hearing the next few sentences, but as a wise person once said, "reiteration is the key to success." Actually, we just made that up. This little section is a reiteration of the "*Does Your Accountant Know Cannabis*" portion of Chapter 3. It should make more sense now that you have read through the processes required to make this happen:

For a producer/ manufacturer, the only way to get <u>any</u> deductions is to allocate expenses to the Cost of Goods Sold by correctly doing inventory/ accrual/ cost accounting. The only way to get <u>all</u> available deductions is to perform this on a recurring basis and by issuing financial statements in accordance with Generally Accepted Accounting Principles at least quarterly if not monthly. Financial statements are typically your balance sheet, income statement (P&L), and statement of cash flows.

Now think of the financial statements as a snapshot in time. Let's say you are a grower/ cultivator, and you are issuing your March 31st financial statements. You must follow the tax laws for inventories (we already discussed § 471) to get your cannabis COGS into these financial statements. You need to know the status of your inventory; how much is raw materials (seeds/ clones, etc.) how much is work in progress (think growing plants), how much is finished goods available for sale (back from the lab and packaged), and how much was sold (COGS). How do you accomplish this? Your state will likely dictate the inventory system you use (Metrc, Arisoft, MJ Freeway, etc.), and your accountant will be at the mercy of that inventory system's accuracy which is unacceptable if the system doesn't match physical inventory. So, a physical inventory of each strain must be performed, and it must be aligned with the time period estimated for the growth of said strain. For instance, you have some OG Bubba Kush that takes 120 days from clone to sale to the dispensary. On March 31st, it's week 7 of 9 in flower, and you need another 3 weeks to cure, dry, trim, test, package and deliver it to the dispensary. So, you are 85 days into the 120 for your OG Bubba Kush. That's 71% complete. 71% of the costs of this crop are allocated to work-in-process inventory for the purposes of your cost accounting. Still a pain in the rear.

Dispensary Example of a Tax Strategy to Capture all Available COGS

The following is another reiteration derived from a portion of Chapter 3, "Why do I Need a Cannabis CPA?":

We know that § 280E means no deductions are available in our industry; however, we also know we can effectively "write off" our Cost of Goods Sold (COGS). At the dispensary this is the cost of acquiring the cannabis products and may include the overhead and activities associated with storing, packaging, and making products ready for sale.

"Trafficking" is the mechanism that inflicts § 280E upon us. Trafficking is when your Budtender sells marijuana to your patient/ client. You cannot deduct the salary for that Budtender when they are doing the trafficking, but you may be able to deduct the salary for the employee working in the back room of your dispensary who is breaking down pounds into eighths and repackaging them for sale or making pre-rolled joints. Now think about the supervisor of both the lab-coat-wearing guy in the back and the Budtender. Assuming this supervisor has no other duties, half of his/ her salary, benefits, etc. would be § 280E and non-deductible, and the other half could be deductible with proper cannabis accounting as he/ she is supervising the guy in the lab coat whose duty is to make the goods ready for sale (COGS).

Using reasonable and consistent methodologies for allocations in accordance with the IRS's rules gives us a bit of control over how we make allocations to COGS. You must also be able to justify the allocations with documentation, i.e., time-sheets, job descriptions, standard operating procedures, pay-stubs, etc.

When an IRS Auditor is doing a walk-through of your facility with you and your representative (you'll want audit representation in the form of a CPA or tax lawyer), it should be easy to distinguish between the Budtender and the back-room worker. If they both look like they are interchangeable and do both trafficking and non-trafficking tasks, they may both be trafficking in the eyes of the auditor. If you outfit a Budtender at the point-of-sale location with a hot pink shirt that has "Budtender" on it, and in the back-room, out of sight from patrons, the dude in the lab coat is rolling joints with a hair net on, the auditor may perceive that you have a COGS room, a COGS employee repackaging product, and accept your tax write-offs. That back-room employee reduces your taxes when he is performing this function. The supervisor's salary allocated to that employee also reduces your tax burden. The 25% of the rent and utilities for that 250 square feet of your 1000 square foot dispensary (250/1000 = 25%) is also a deduction, and so on. The way you plan your facility design and your Standard Operating Procedures (SOPs) clearly impacts your bottom line. By now, we are sure you get the picture.

CHAPTER 12 – STATE INCOME AND OTHER TAXES UNDER § 280E

§ 280E applies to the taxation of income in most states; however, it may vary between corporations and individuals. The next chapter is on this topic, but it is relevant to point out that C Corporations are essentially another "person" for tax purposes, while entities such as sole proprietorships, partnerships, and S-Corporations will essentially "pass-through" their income to the tax return of the individual or shareholder (in the case of the S Corp). LLCs are disregarded by the IRS, so if you set up an LLC you will be taxed by default as a sole proprietor or partnership unless you affirmatively elect to be taxed as an S-Corp or C Corp.

Why does this matter here? Because in several states, § 280E applies on the corporate but not the individual level, but in California, for example, the opposite is true. The crux of the matter is that we need to be cognizant of how each state might or might not apply § 280E and to whom it applies. Note that the following may not be up to date and is always subject to change as laws change:

States where § 280E is not applied to Corporations:

- AR, CA, CO, HI, OR

States where § 280E is not applied to Individuals:

- AK, AR, CO, HI, NH, NJ, OR, PA

Sales, Excise and Local Taxes

It is a significant and necessary undertaking to develop a thorough understanding of all the taxes that apply to activities and transactions for each of your cannabis businesses. The taxation of state legal marijuana businesses is often drilled down to the level of the exact location of the business itself. This obviously makes the location of the business an area of due diligence to assign to your tax and legal professionals. For instance, AmeriCann, Inc. broke ground on the largest medical marijuana facility in America in 2018 and agreed to provide the town of Freetown, Massachusetts with a $1 for every square foot built. This is essentially a one-time million-dollar tax! Cities, towns and municipalities tax at various rates and by various methods (i.e. building square feet vs plot of land). In some states, medical marijuana is not subject to sales or excise tax, in others it is subject to one or the other, and in many states, it is subject to both taxes. Most states have sales and excise tax on recreational marijuana, but Maine has sales tax on both medical and recreational but no excise tax on either. In contrast, Alaska has excise tax on both medical and recreational but no sales tax on either.

An eighth can cost nearly 25% more in Seattle than in Las Vegas. Customers should be made aware that they could pay about 18 (Vegas) to 45% (Seattle) more than the sticker price at the register. Retailers should include the tax breakdown on receipts to provide transparency to customers.

You will need a procedure and order for how you apply taxes, as some will be required to compound on top of others. For instance, excise tax and local tax may be added to the product's sales price after the state sales tax has already applied. Effectively a tax on tax.

Whether Cannabis is legal or not, some states levy a "Stamp Tax" or "Controlled Substance Tax." Dealers in illegal drugs purchase, typically from their Department of Revenue, and may be required to affix these stamps to the products they sell. States that have such programs include: AL, CT, GA, ID, IL, IA, KS, KY, LA, MA, MN, NE, NC, OK, RI, SC, TN.

Are we wondering why we got in the legal cannabis industry yet?

Excise Tax under § 280E – CCA 201531016

As mentioned earlier, we have some guidance from the IRS Chief Counsel on the treatment of marijuana excise taxes. Effectively, you won't get taxed via § 280E for the excise taxes you collect and remit to the state when wholesale or retail sales are made. Specifically, this memorandum deals with the treatment of excise tax levied by the State of Washington but may be applied to all state excise taxes. The following excerpt is what we rely upon to be able to reduce the amount realized on the sale of cannabis by excise taxes imposed under state laws:

> "Accordingly, pursuant to § 164(a), a taxpayer who paid the marijuana excise tax should treat the expenditure as a reduction in the amount realized on the sale of the property rather than as either a part of the inventoriable cost of that property or a deduction from gross income.1 Though § 280E prohibits deductions and credits for these businesses, this excise tax is neither a deduction from gross income nor a tax credit. Consequently, § 280E does not preclude a taxpayer from accounting for this excise tax as a reduction in the amount realized on the sale of the property."

Part V: Choice of Business Entity

CHAPTER 13 – CANNABIS OVERVIEW

"Annual income twenty pounds, annual expenditure nineteen six, result happiness. Annual income twenty pounds, annual expenditure twenty pound ought and six, result misery." - *Charles Dickens*

The above Charles Dickens quote is appropriate, as § 280E in combination with your choice of entity selection can be the difference between happiness and misery in the cannabis space. Selecting the wrong entity for your particular business and personal financial situations can also force Scrooge-like spending habits upon you during the holidays.

You will need a knowledgeable cannabis attorney. We repeat, you will need a knowledgeable cannabis attorney working together with your CPA to get this right in terms of your legal and financial needs as an individual and as a business. Here, more than in any other circumstance, the advice you would normally receive from a tax or legal professional is counterintuitive when applied to the cannabis industry. Never mind the usual concerns that legal and accounting professionals must consider when deciding on the choice of entity; aside from the new tax laws, § 280E is the other 800-pound gorilla in the room. Due to the punitive nature of § 280E, tax liabilities, as shown in Table 2 of chapter 8, can eliminate what would otherwise be a decent profit.

Imagine a cannabis startup where things don't go well. The business ends up with a tax liability of $300,000 despite breaking even from a profit and loss perspective. This is not possible with a "normal" business, but this is a cannabis touching business that creates what we call "phantom income." Sounds scary, right? You didn't make any money, but you were disallowed so many deductions by § 280E that by the IRS's calculations you had plenty of taxable income. So, they tax it. Say the owners decide to close its doors due to the excessive disallowance of deductions by § 280E that put them in the hole. The potential for these circumstances in the start-up phase of a cannabis business tends to lead tax advisors to suggest a C Corporation. The reason is, the properly implemented C Corporation will shield the owners of this money-losing business from personal liability for that $300,000 tax bill, as a C Corporation is treated as taxpayer separate from the individual shareholders. Pass-through entities (simple LLC, S-Corp, partnership, sole proprietorship) may leave you holding the bag. While this book offers no legal advice (we are not lawyers), it is important that those who advise you on entity selection take § 280E into account due to these unique circumstances.

Entity selection and the way assets are inserted into the entity to get it up and running may also have unintended consequences for spouses. A sole proprietor wife simply using an LLC to house her cannabis grow operation and funding her canna-business bank account (if she was lucky enough to get one) from her joint account with her husband could drag him into her potential § 280E tax liability mess and potential banking issues if they file a joint tax return. If you are thinking of getting married or are married filing separately and starting a cannabis business, you may want to evaluate the situation with your tax advisor and lawyer before you switch to married filing jointly.

Once again, no two instances are the same. As we mentioned earlier, if you are a Corporation in California, you are not subject to § 280E on your state tax return (you still are on your federal return); however, if you are a pass-through entity (LLC, S Corp, Sole proprietor, Partnership), § 280E applies. The opposite is true in various other states <scratches head>.

Let's look at the characteristics of various entities.

Entity Types

C Corporation

First, understand that there is a difference between a legal C Corporation and forming an LLC that elects to be taxed as a C Corporation. The former provides a specified legal protection and the latter gets you the tax treatment that we discuss here. We would need a lawyer to address the difference between an LLC taxed as a C and a straight up C Corp in each state, so we're not going to go there. A C Corporation is a separate tax entity, meaning that the C Corporation first pays taxes at a flat rate of 21% (2018), and then dividends are distributed and are taxed at the owner level (this is called "double-taxation"), generally as qualified dividends, at 0%, then 15%, then 20% tax rates as your income level rises. There is also the possibility of an additional 3.8% net investment income tax on top of the 20% if you are doing well. You can also be an employee of your C Corporation and pay yourself a reasonable salary subject to payroll taxes at the corporate and individual level, then pay ordinary income tax on your wages. You don't need to have a firm grasp on these concepts, but your cannabis attorneys and CPAs should.

If you are looking to shield yourself from personal liability or grow into a massive corporation with investors, a C Corp may be the right choice. A highly profitable and expanding business that would put an individual in a high tax bracket, say making $700,000 and in a 35% tax bracket, may be better off as a C Corp, as it may be acquiring capital (by selling stock) to expand. A C Corp can also sell stock to an unlimited number of investors and have multiple classes of stock (an S Corp is limited to 100 investors and one class of stock). Also note that C Corps can elect to be taxed as a pass-through S Corp. C Corps file IRS Form 1120 at the end of the year and must maintain many formalities to remain in corporate solution, such as meeting minutes. Normal C Corps can take Net Operating Loss deductions (NOLs) in bad years, but cannabis companies cannot due to § 280E. Remember, this is a broad overview; there are stacks of three-inch thick books on how C Corps operate, and most haven't been updated for the new Tax Cuts and Jobs Act (TJCA).

§ 1202 – Partial Exclusion of Gain from Certain Small Business Stock

Speaking of the TCJA and corporations, the 21% corporate tax rate rejuvenates IRC § 1202 which gives a potentially huge tax break to people (not corporations) who hold onto their C Corporation stock. If you plan to have a valuable business, there may be an advantage to be had by issuing your stock from a C Corporation. § 1202 has the potential to exclude 50% of your gain on the sale of the stock from capital gains tax if you hold your shares for 5 years and meet applicable criteria, such as it being a small business (assets less than $50,000,000) and not being on a laundry list of specified business types that need not apply (like accounting firms ☹).

Farming is excluded, so whether indoor cultivators need apply would be a talking point for the attorney you use to create your entity – this hasn't been litigated that we know of, but manufacturers will certainly want to have this discussion before selecting a pass-through entity or electing to have their C Corp taxed as an S Corp. If a start-up business is operated as an S corporation, the founders will not be able to convert the business to a C corporation in order to take advantage of Qualified Small Business Stock (QSBS) treatment for their previously issued stock. A corporation must be a C corporation when the stock is issued. Note also that stock acquired after the conversion of an S corporation *may* qualify as QSBS.

Sole Proprietorship

Sole proprietorships are risky if you are in the cannabis business. You have no limit to your liability and profits or losses and tax liabilities pass through to the first page of your individual 1040 return by way of Schedule C. If business loss exceeds other income, individual can carry forward NOLs indefinitely in a normal business, but we are talking cannabis, so once again § 280E bites you.

Partnerships

This is another pass-through entity which files IRS Form 1065 for information only – the partner's distributive share of partnership income/ loss passes through to the individual's return via Form K-1. The Operating Agreement dictates the terms of the partnership. There is unlimited personal liability for acts of the partnership or partner acting on behalf of partnership (joint and several liability). Partnerships dissolve upon death, bankruptcy, or incapacity of a partner, so it is a structure that is probably not a good choice for a cannabis company.

S Corporation (Subchapter S)

S Corporations are pass-through entities that file Form 1120S. They must meet specific criteria to remain an S Corporation. Only individuals, estates, and certain trusts may be shareholders, so if you're looking to get investors, you won't be able to have a C Corp or partnership fund you. There are some formalities in having an S Corp, and you must run payroll and pay the owners a reasonable salary before paying any dividends. S Corps are traditionally used to reduce self-employment taxes that might otherwise be paid by a partnership or sole proprietorship turning at least a modest profit.

Loughman v. Commissioner – S Corporation Double Taxation – Oops!

In a 2018 Tax Court Memorandum Opinion (not precedent setting) regarding the case of *Loughman v. Commissioner*, an S Corporation felt the full burn of § 280 E. The Loughman duo, owners and sole shareholders of a Colorado dispensary, paid themselves a salary for working in their business. Normally, an S Corporation deducts W-2 wages paid to employees and/ or owners performing services for the business. The Loughman's were the only employees of their S Corp, and the IRS determined that § 280 E disallowed deductions for a majority of their activities (trafficking) as employees/ managers of the dispensary. This caused the Loughman's to be double-taxed. As the owners of the S Corp, the disallowed salary deductions created phantom income that passed through to their individual tax returns. Then, as employees, their W-2 wages were taxed and subject to Self-Employment taxes. They tried to argue before the Tax Court that they were discriminated against for being an S Corp; however, the court reminded them that they chose to make the election. Note that in a cultivation operation, the impact would not be as significant.

LLC (Limited Liability Company)

An LLC is statutory, meaning that it is not a tax entity as all the above are, but it is a status granted by the state that limits the liability of a sole proprietor, partnership, S Corporation, or an entity electing to be taxed as a corporation. An LLC with one member is typically a disregarded entity in the eyes of the IRS (a sole proprietor) and one with two or more partners is generally classified as a partnership.

Multiple Entities

Time and again we get questions about what we like to call "musical entities." "Management company" this, and "holding company" that. "Real estate company" this, and "§ 280 E company" that. Once again, this is a conversation to be had with an attorney, as there are valid legal reasons to establish, for instance, a holding company with separate real estate, management, cultivation, and dispensary companies underneath it. Emphasis on legal reasons! The IRS looks at substance over form for tax purposes, meaning that if you think you can set up multiple legal entities to skirt § 280 E, you may be creating nothing more than "sham transactions" (IRS terminology).

"Substance over form" is tax law doctrine that requires transactions to have a substantial purpose aside from reducing Federal taxes and to have a profit motive aside from the tax effect. In addition, the business purpose doctrine effectively requires a substantial business purpose for a transaction other than avoiding or reducing Federal tax. These concepts arose from a Supreme Court case from 1935 (*Gregory v. Helvering*). The IRS relies on this case law when analyzing your financial statements to determine whether you have failed to honor either doctrine. Your financial statements should "give a complete, relevant, and accurate picture of transactions and events." Furthermore, if you are creating transactions among businesses that you have a stake in for the purpose of avoidance or reducing taxes, the IRS has the authority to and has been known to deny any tax benefits that arose. As it may take up to a few years for the IRS to unveil these transactions, you may be subject to penalties and interest as well as back taxes.

Many vertically integrated cannabis companies or separate companies with at least one shared owner may have what are essentially "inter-company transactions" (i.e. cultivator to dispensary, management company to cultivator, etc.). This is when the same parties or parties that are not at arm's length (a.k.a. related parties) buy from/ sell to each other. The IRS can rely upon IRC § 482 to redistribute among groups or individuals the dollar amounts of those transactions in the way that would most clearly reflect how the transaction would have occurred if it were undertaken with an unrelated 3rd party. Part of avoiding scrutiny in these transactions might entail, as an example, keeping documentation of what market prices are for wholesale cannabis products that you are transferring to your retail company.

In any transaction among related parties or establishment of another business entity, ask yourself if you set up the legal entity or set up a transaction between companies to obtain deductions that would otherwise be disallowed by § 280E. If your answer is yes, there is a good chance you will not come out of an IRS audit unscathed. We would expect the IRS to take notice of a company that has only income but no expenses and that pays a company with only expenses but no income. If you set up a shell company with a building and the necessary equipment to cultivate or manufacture cannabis products, you may be subject to § 280E. If you have made loans to a cannabis touching company with an option to convert to equity, this may be subject to § 280E. On the other hand, if you are a landlord/ property management company with absolutely no involvement in the cultivator's business, you have a good argument that you should not be subject to § 280E. As always, consult with cannabis attorneys and CPAs on all matters regarding business entity.

Part VI: CBD

CHAPTER 14 – CONFUSION ABOUT TAXATION OF CBD (UPDATE 12/2018)

CBD/ industrial hemp is legal if produced in accordance with the law, but at the same time could be subject to § 280E if deemed Schedule I by the IRS. The interpretation of whether "industrial hemp" and its derivatives are Schedule I depends on who you ask and could change any day (with pending legislation). In September 2018, an Administrative Law Judge with the U.S. Postal service finally ruled in favor of the mailability of CBD that is protected by the 2014 Farm Bill, stating that it is not Schedule I. It took this long just to figure out if you can ship CBD, but the Postal Service's decision has no impact on the IRS's interpretation of the matter.

The Agricultural Act of 2014 also known as the 2014 Farm Bill expired on September 30th, 2018. At the time of this writing, we are waiting on proposed legislation which would legalize the cultivation of all industrial hemp and *potentially* legalize *all* hemp derived CBD. The Hemp Farming Act of 2018 is attached to the 2018 Farm Bill and, if passed, may remove cannabis that does not exceed 0.3% THC from Schedule I of the Controlled

Substances Act, adding it to the mundane list of agricultural commodities. This would potentially relieve all industrial hemp and its derivatives (CBD) from the perils of § 280E.

Where do we stand in the meantime? In muddy waters, unfortunately. Let's start with the facts. The DEA issued a directive on May 22, 2018 to acknowledge that the 2014 Farm Bill preempts the Controlled Substances Act where the two conflict. Therefore, "*industrial hemp*" that is cultivated pursuant to a state pilot program is protected by the 2014 Farm Bill, and any derived CBD would be protected as well. Most states (41 at present) have laws that allow the growing of industrial hemp under such a program.

We can turn to the law that codified the 2014 Farm Bill, 7 U.S. Code § 5940 - Legitimacy of industrial hemp research, to see that it is legal to grow industrial hemp which is cultivated pursuant to a state-permitted agricultural pilot program or in an institution of higher education for the purpose of researching the growth, cultivation, or marketing of industrial hemp. The DEA conceded, and the Court agreed, that the Farm Bill of 2014 supersedes the DEA's authority under the Controlled Substances Act as it relates to hemp. The first line of this section § 5940, however, begins, "Notwithstanding the Controlled Substances Act" – can you see where we are going with this? Sure, its legal to grow industrial hemp and extract CBD from it, but "*notwithstanding*" effectively means *despite* the Controlled Substances Act. The 2014 Farm Bill does not explicitly remove industrial hemp from Schedule I, but it does provide a legal work-around. As we know, § 280E applies to Schedule I. Some will argue that since the 2014 Farm Bill preempts the CSA, then industrial hemp is no longer Schedule I. The DEA, on the other hand, correctly points out that, "Section 7706 (of the 2014 Farm Bill) did not remove industrial hemp from the controlled substances list." As a result, Congress issued an Amicus brief supporting the Hemp Industries Association in their case against the DEA, conveying that the intent of the 2014 Farm Bill was to prompt the DEA to effect the administrative changes necessary to remove industrial hemp from the CSA. The DEA has not done so to date but has clarified in a May 22, 2018 internal directive that their intent is not to target cannabinoids (a.k.a. CBD), but to enforce only those products which fall under their definition of "marijuana." Their definition of marijuana does not align with the 2014 Farm Bill's "not to exceed 0.3%" guidance. While the DEA excludes the mature stalks and sterile seeds from the definition of "marijuana," they contend that CBD can only be produced from the parts of the plant which are defined as "marijuana" under the Controlled Substances Act. Specifically, the DEA relies upon outdated (1970's) scientific literature that suggests that cannabinoids (CBD) can only be derived in excess of parts per million from the illegal parts of the plant. This leads some to contend that industrial hemp is still subject to § 280E and suggest that you should tread lightly with the IRS. Auditors may not adopt the position that the expired 2014 Farm Bill removes hemp and hemp derived CBD from Schedule I.

Congress's intent is manifested again in The Consolidated Appropriations Act of 2017, which asserts that federal funding may not be used

> "to prohibit the transportation, processing, sale, or use of industrial hemp that is grown or cultivated in accordance with section 7606 of the Agricultural Act of 2014, within or outside the State in which the industrial hemp is grown or cultivated."

Said another way, CBD derived from hemp farming activities conducted in full compliance with state pilot programs is federally legal in all 50 states. It seems that hemp/ CBD may be legal and Schedule I at the same time!

Some CBD is always subject to § 280E. First, understand that hemp and marijuana are one and the same; both are the genus *cannabis sativa*. To demonize the plant, some government folks in the 1930s forced their anti-immigration sentiment on the plant by calling it by its Mexican name, "marihuana." CBD may be derived from either marijuana or hemp. There is a common misconception that <u>all</u> CBD is federally legal and can be shipped across state lines if it does not exceed 0.3% THC. On the contrary, not all CBD is federally legal and not all states have adopted industrial hemp programs. CBD derived from "marijuana" is always Schedule I per the DEA as there is no argument to be made relying on the 2014 Farm Bill. This would require the IRS to subject it to § 280E and necessitate that it be sold pursuant to state laws at the state legal level (while it remains federally illegal).

In addition, a court case by the name of *Hemp Industries Association v. DEA* resulted in the exclusion of imported "non-psychoactive hemp" from the Controlled Substances Act. Also, CBD derived from what the DEA considers to be the legal parts of the cannabis plant is legal. Take this to mean that the sterilized seeds, oil or cake made from the seeds, and mature stalks are not controlled by the Controlled Substances Act. This is why you can buy hemp seeds at your local grocery store. The DEA argues that it is impossible to create CBD in significant quantities from these parts of the plant, which leads to more conflict. The DEA stands by a rule specifically targeting CBD, industrial hemp derived or not, in stating that any "extract containing one or more cannabinoids that has been derived from any plant of the genus cannabis" is considered a Schedule I. Yes, the 2014 Farm Bill preempts this, but "notwithstanding the Controlled Substances Act" does not exempt CBD from Schedule I and § 280E, right?

There is a way in which CBD can dodge § 280E, and only one drug falls into this category to date. The DEA agreed that only Food and Drug Administration (FDA) approved drugs with a CBD ingredient that contain less than 0.1% THC will automatically be moved to Schedule V of the CSA. The DEA has rescheduled a single CBD drug from I to V per the FDA's approval to date, Epidiolex, which treats epilepsy. Currently, the DEA cannot remove CBD products from being scheduled altogether due to a 47-year-old revision of an international treaty, the *Single Convention on Narcotic Drugs.* An irrelevant side note: this means that in states where marijuana is not legal, a patient would technically need a prescription for CBD to be in compliance with state and federal law.

Whether CBD or industrial hemp is subject to § 280E or not, keep in mind that the IRS lives in the past (it may take years before you are audited) and applies the tax laws as written in the years being audited. In other words, ignoring § 280E in 2016-2018 can catch up to you in 2019 even if the punitive tax laws no longer apply to CBD in the future. For this reason, ensure you have documentation to support the origin of your legal CBD products, or take care of your tax liability under § 280E for your federally illegal CBD product sales. If you are in the gray area, it would be prudent to maintain your inventories via the rules for inventories under IRC § 471, so even if § 280E comes back to bite you, you have the documentation to get some COGS deductions.

Part VII: The IRS, Audits and Banking

CHAPTER 15 – THE IRS AND TAX LAW

"...the right to pay no more than the correct amount of tax"

- Taxpayer Bill of Rights

Did you know the IRS studies areas of perceived noncompliance and allocates audit resources accordingly?

The IRS has instituted CIP (Compliance Initiative Projects) which are projects designed to identify, measure, or analyze taxpayer noncompliance. They study or analyze groups of individuals, businesses such as those within an occupation, industry, geographic area or specific economic activity or event. You guessed it; they are gathering data and using it to analyze tax compliance specifically for California cannabis operations (word on the street is that they already hit Colorado cannabis businesses based on a lack of timely filed Form 8300s – 8300s are discussed at length in chapter 18).

The IRS aggressively pursues the cannabis business due to the cash intensive nature of the industry, and likely due to the pervasiveness of errors made with respect to proper application of § 280E. By identifying perceived weaknesses in the industry and shoring them up at your cannabis business, you will be less susceptible to any Compliance Initiative Project that may come your way.

In this part of the book, we will gloss over the IRS's responsibilities to you, your responsibilities to the IRS, how you are more susceptible to audits due to the nature of your industry, and the requirements of the Bank Secrecy Act.

Taxpayer Bill of Rights

In 2014, the IRS rehashed the rights that you always had, and put them in an easy to understand, one-page document that is worth printing and keeping handy: https://www.irs.gov/pub/irs-pdf/p5170.pdf

There is a link at the bottom of the page to the IRS's Taxpayer Advocate site. We want you to know that these programs exist, and we'll summarize the Taxpayer Bill of Rights in some bullet points:

- Most importantly, you have "the right to pay no more than the correct amount of tax" due (including penalties and interest) – this is why you will want to properly apply IRC § 471 to your cannabis inventory and issue GAAP financials contemporaneously, so you don't pay a penny more in taxes than is legally due.

- You have the "right to retain representation" when dealing with the IRS; if you cannot afford representation, you may seek assistance from the Low-Income Taxpayer Clinic.

    - Who can represent you before the IRS, you ask?

        - A Certified Public Accountant (CPA), Attorney, Enrolled Agent (EA), Enrolled Actuary or any other person permitted to represent a taxpayer before IRS

- The IRS is to provide explanations on decisions they made about your tax account and issue clear guidance on what you need to do to be compliant.
- The IRS is trying to be prompt, courteous and professional when you contact them, and if they aren't, you can ask to speak to a supervisor.
- The IRS is required to notify you when they finish an audit and how much time you have to challenge their position. They must let you know how long they have to audit a tax year or collect a tax debt.
- You can object to IRS decisions, provide more information and your reasons, and expect the IRS to consider your position and respond to you if they disagree, at which point you can appeal their decision through an independent Office of Appeals. Generally, you have the right to take your case to court.
- You have the right to privacy and confidentiality.
- The tax system is to be fair and just. The Taxpayer Advocate Service is available for those with financial difficulties or difficulty resolving tax issues with the IRS in a timely manner.
-

Tax Due Dates

This is in no way an all-inclusive tax calendar. We cover just a few of the most common filing dates. For specific forms, you or your accountant will need to verify the due dates in IRS Publication 509 (Google it) or via the IRS's online tax calendar https://www.tax.gov/calendar/. The dates below don't scratch the surface for employers, farmers, and certain others in particular, so treat this as a list of a few of the more notable dates to remember.

January 31st

IRS Form 1099s are to be issued by January 31st. If you made payments to contractors or for other specified expenses in aggregate of $600 or more during the tax year in the course of your trade or business, you will need to issue 1099s. You can search the web for the IRS's *General Instructions for Certain Information Returns* and the specific instructions, such as *Instructions for Form 1099-MISC* to determine which forms are required. Similarly, you should be receiving 1099s from other parties that you do business with when they are required to issue them.

April 15th

We all know that the Form 1040 filing deadline for individuals and sole proprietors (or a single member LLC) is typically April 15th but may be pushed back due to weekends or holidays. You can file for a six-month extension via Form 4868 by this date, but if you owe any tax liability, it is to be paid by the April due date to avoid penalties and interest.

March 15th

Partnership (Form 1065) and S-Corporation (Form 1120S) returns are due a month before the individual returns which they flow through to. The six-month extension is also applicable to these returns via Form 7004.

Corporations

The following is directly from IRS Publication 509, as the timeline for corporations is not straight-forward: Form 1120 (or Form 7004 to extend). This form is due on the 15th day of the 4th month after the end of the corporation's tax year. However, a corporation with a fiscal tax year ending June 30 must file by the 15th day of the 3rd month after the end of its tax year. A corporation with a short tax year ending anytime in June will be treated as if the short year ended on June 30, and must file by the 15th day of the 3rd month after the end of its tax year.

Estimated tax payments

Estimated tax payments (Form 1040-ES) are generally for those who don't have withholding or who expect a tax liability of $1,000 or more at the end of the year. Pub 509 states, "Payments are due on the 15th day of the 4th, 6th, and 9th months of your tax year and on the 15th day of the 1st month after your tax year ends."

- Note: This is not quarterly as in every three months.

- Due dates are April 15th, June 15th, September 15th and January 15th of the following year.

Payroll taxes
The IRS looks back at your Form 941s (the quarterly wage and tax return) for the twelve-month period ending the preceding June 30th to determine whether you must submit payroll tax deposits quarterly, monthly, biweekly or semi-weekly. IRS Publication 15 (Circular E – Employer's Tax Guide) is where you start for payroll.

IRS Penalties

Criminal penalties can be handed down from the Department of Justice (not the IRS) for tax fraud or aiding and abetting another in committing tax fraud. Tax fraud is intentionally filing materially false tax returns. The convicted may be subject to forfeiture of property and/or jail time.

There is much more minutia we could cover, such as minimum penalties for each month an S Corp or partnership return is late even if you don't owe, multiplied by number of shareholders/ partners, etc., but these are the significant **civil** penalties you should be aware of:

- Frivolous Return – $5,000 (this basically means in bad faith)
- Negligence – 20% of portion of the tax underpayment attributed to negligence
- Civil Fraud – 75% of portion of the tax return attributable to fraud
- Failure to file – 5% of tax due per month, maximum 25%
- Failure to pay – 0.5% per month each month tax is unpaid, maximum 25%
- Estimated tax – No penalty will apply for 2018 if taxpayer pays lesser of 90% of current year's tax liability or 100% of the prior year's liability (or 110% of 2017 if Adjusted Gross Income [AGI] over $150,000). This penalty is an interest rate set by the IRS on a quarterly basis (currently around 5%)

- 100% penalty on unpaid withholding taxes – if you don't withhold income and social security taxes on wages paid to employees and promptly pay the government, the penalty is assessed at 100% of the amount not paid. The IRS has seized business owners' homes for this!
- Accuracy-related penalties – 20-40% of the increase in assessed tax depending upon circumstances
- There are also federal excise tax penalties, penalties for failure to provide foreign information, penalties for tax advisers, and more!

CHAPTER 16 – AUDITS AND COMPLIANCE

Introduction

When it comes to the IRS, good defense is your offense. Document, document, document! File the required forms on time, every time. Have invoices and receipts and records to substantiate all transactions, cash or otherwise. Establish internal controls; ensure restricted access to cash and inventory, segregation of duties as appropriate, and inventory and cash controls are in place. Be wary of any transactions that just don't feel right, and properly file IRS Form 8300s when transacting with cash. We recommend that you seek a compliance expert/ consultant/ lawyer to manage compliance as regulations at various levels and in various locations need to be addressed by those well-versed in that area. When GreenBeanCFO obtains a client in a new jurisdiction, we conduct the due diligence necessary to understand the regulatory landscape surrounding that business. We also suggest the implementation of a digital checklist/ playbook to include links to state websites, cannabis business startup guides, and anything that can help keep you up to date and informed.

Willfully failing to file taxes is one extreme we discuss in this chapter, but there are many ways where complacency alone can destroy your business and your finances; just look at the Alterman case (chapter 17). We strongly urge you to consider the need to consult with representation if you learn that you are being audited, as the IRS uses complex guides to do deep dives into your business and possibly your life. Their conviction rate in criminal cases is far north of 90%.

Prison for Dispensary Owner Infiltrated by Undercover IRS Agents

On September 17, 2018, a federal judge sentenced Matthew Price to seven months in federal prison for willfully failing to file tax returns between 2011 and 2014 (The IRS has a long memory). Mr. Price is the owner of Cannabliss & Co., a legal Portland, Oregon-based medical marijuana dispensary. Upon completion of his prison sentence, Price will be on supervised release for three years with six months of home detention. He was also ordered to pay the IRS $262,776 in restitution, a majority of which he paid before sentencing.

The IRS initially investigated Price for not paying employment taxes for his employees. According to an undercover IRS agent posing as a potential employee, the agent approached Price and in conversation, Price stated that he didn't want to "*get ripped*" in taxes (by putting employees on payroll), and also disclosed that he was using the money from his business for personal uses. This prompted further investigation which revealed the failure to file tax returns.

Cannabliss's Income ranged from approximately $42,000 to $590,000 per year as the initially modest operation gained traction. Ironically, although Price helped the OLCC (Oregon Liquor Control Commission) write the regulations for the state's cannabis industry, he failed to follow regulations. At the time of this writing, Mr. Price's ability to operate in the Oregon cannabis industry upon completion of his sentence is being debated by regulators.

Commingling business and personal funds will get you in trouble with the IRS. In Price's case, the commingled business proceeds were used for personal purchases, including an expensive sports car, Portland Trailblazers tickets, and a Rolex. His defense was that he wasn't sure what he could deduct, what records to keep, and that his accountants weren't dependable. The court wasn't buying it. The judge acknowledged that while Mr. Price did not "walk into this with an MBA," he was intelligent enough to be aware of "one of the most basic obligations of running a business," paying taxes. Ignorance is not Cannabliss (sorry).

As an entrepreneur in an industry with rules that are changing daily, don't make the mistake of procrastinating when it comes to the least exciting part of your business - paying your federal, state and local taxes, paying payroll taxes and keeping good records. Keep your business and personal accounts separate. Comingling your accounts can also *pierce the corporate veil*, meaning that you may lose any liability protection provided by your LLC or other business entity. File your returns on time. If you haven't been 100% compliant thus far, fix it now before a federal prosecutor fixes it for you.

The IRS's Cash Intensive Business Audit Techniques Guide (ATG)

Cannabis touching businesses operating or having operated in the past on a cash basis (bags of money in hand) are not only more likely to be audited, but audits will be done in accordance with the IRS's Cash Intensive Businesses Audit Technique Guide. If this applies to your business, you should peruse the guide on the IRS's website:

- https://www.irs.gov/businesses/small-businesses-self-employed/cash-intensive-businesses-audit-techniques-guide-table-of-contents

It's intuitive that the IRS will want to see that your books are aligned with your income, but this exhaustive audit guide demonstrates how an IRS auditor can lead you to rabbit-holes that you don't want to go down. We are only scratching the surface in this chapter; however, be wary of what you could be up against. IRS examiners may interview you, your family, and third parties. They'll ask you to walk them through your business operations, internal controls, your other businesses, and if you have a hoard of cash, they'll want to trace it to its source. They may tour your facility and might even ask you if you have a second safe in your home. They will investigate all your accounts: personal, business, investments, etc. Business ratios may be analyzed, and explanations may be sought for significant changes in, for example, profit margins, inventory turnover, etc.

Let's cover some highlights of the process outlined by the audit guide:

- The Audit Technique Guide (ATG) suggests the auditor take the following general course of action:
    - Establish a likeliness of underreported or unreported income
    - Request an explanation of discrepancies from the taxpayer (you)
    - If you can't or won't explain discrepancies, Financial Status Audit Techniques (FSAT) may be required
- An FSAT is an analysis to estimate whether your reported cash flow covers your expenses – both business and personal.
- If your books or records are missing, incomplete, or irregularities are identified, or if your FSAT shows a material imbalance in cash flows after consideration of adjustments identified during the exam, you are likely to be subjected to a more in-depth analysis.
- If the IRS documents evidence that establishes the likelihood of unreported income, they may proceed to the "**formal indirect method**" to determine the actual tax liability. You don't want to put yourself in a position where the IRS is calculating the tax you should have paid – this can lead to fines, penalties, a huge tax liability, the shutdown of your business, and possibly hard time in the joint!

What You Should be Thinking About NOW to be Prepared for an Audit

- Simply stated, **document, document, document**. Maintain bullet-proof, accessible books and records. Identify and clean up any past weaknesses.

- Hire competent cannabis accountants and lawyers who insist that everything is done in accordance with state and federal laws and IRS best practices.

- You want to be able to provide all relevant information directly to the IRS, so they are less likely to contact third parties; discrepancies among parties can lead to a deeper dive into your life.

- Consult with your lawyer/ CPA to have a game plan in place in the event of an audit. Heed this quote directly from the ATG:

    - "Respect the taxpayer's right to representation. Examiners cannot require that a taxpayer participate in the audit or be interviewed without a summons. However, examiners need to talk with a knowledgeable person. If needed, the taxpayer's voluntary presence at an interview, or tour of the business site, can be requested through the representative."

- Be familiar with some of the more obvious triggers of the formal indirect method:

<u>**From the IRS:**</u>
4.10.4.6.2.1 (05-27-2011)
When to Use a Formal Indirect Method

1. The use of a formal indirect method to make the actual determination of tax liability should be considered when the factual development of the case leads the examiner to the conclusion that the taxpayer's tax return and supporting books and records do not

accurately reflect the total taxable income received and the examiner has established a reasonable likelihood of unreported income.

2. The following list, which is not intended to be all inclusive, identifies circumstances that, individually or in combination, would support the use of a formal indirect method.

A. A financial status analysis that cannot be balanced; i.e., the taxpayer's known business and personal expenses exceed the reported income per the return and nontaxable sources of funds have not been identified to explain the difference.
B. Irregularities in the taxpayer's books and weak internal controls.
C. Gross profit percentages change significantly from one year to another or are unusually high or low for that market segment or industry.
D. The taxpayer's bank accounts have unexplained items of deposit.
E. The taxpayer does not make regular deposits of income but uses cash instead.
F. A review of the taxpayer's prior and subsequent year returns show a significant increase in net worth not supported by reported income.
G. There are no books and records. Examiners should determine whether books and/or records ever existed, and whether books and records exist for the prior or subsequent years. If books and records have been destroyed, determine who destroyed them, why, and when.
H. No method of accounting has been regularly used by the taxpayer or the method used does not clearly reflect income. See IRC 446(b).

CHAPTER 17 – $469,490 FAIL: ALTERMAN VS. IRS COMMISSIONER

Not only did her Colorado medical marijuana business fail, but Mrs. Alterman and her husband owed the IRS over $469,000 when they walked out of U.S. Tax Court earlier this year.

In June 2018, the *Alterman vs. IRS Commissioner (of the IRS)* case held that Altermeds LLC, a dispensary / cultivator, was "not entitled to any business-expense deductions." The judge also lowered their Cost of Goods Sold (COGS) deduction, and hit them with a bill:

- $391,242 for income tax deficiencies
- $78,248 for accuracy-related penalties attributed to negligence (20% penalty)

According to their books, Altermeds LLC only made $64,534 in net profits over the two years in question, but the owners were now down over $400,000 for that period due to the unique nature of the taxation of cannabis businesses. Medical marijuana businesses are still federally illegal, so Internal Revenue Code § 280E applies – this means NO DEDUCTIONS a.k.a. tax write-offs for business expenses that any normal business would be entitled to.

Sidebar: The good news is that the 16th Amendment of the Constitution allows for taxable income to be reduced by the COGS only if these costs are properly recorded and attributed to inventory (cannabis products in this case). Click here for more on the taxation of cannabis businesses.

Poor record keeping, shoddy books, and a host of other accounting issues led the Tax Court to hold that Altermeds LLC was negligent due to their failure to keep adequate books and records or to substantiate items properly. They could have sought relief if they relied on professional advice about the tax treatment of their business. Although they had bookkeepers and tax preparers, they never sought specific advice regarding proper inventory accounting or the effect of IRC section § 280E. The Tax Court memo stated, "This lack of inquiry evinces their lack of interest in complying with the federal tax laws."

Remember, the taxpayer bears the burden of proving the IRS is incorrect in its findings. This means that you need evidence (accurate records) and a knowledgeable accounting and finance team in place now if you are going to make it through an audit unscathed. Be proactive; cannabis businesses are more likely to be audited by the IRS due to a history of noncompliance.
Selected highlights of Altermed's blunders:

- The IRS recalculated and reduced Altermed's COGS (deductions).
- The court couldn't determine employee wages paid for work performed at the grow site versus the dispensary.
- Altermeds had instances of general ledger purchases of smokable marijuana with the payee being Home Depot or Lowes – they mixed up receipts.
- Altermeds recorded cash taken from the register to purchase marijuana products.
- Alterman paid her son with a check which he cashed and used the cash to buy merchandise for the business.
- Pages were missing from their Visa statements.
- The bookkeeper, when they had one, relied on documents provided by Alterman to do the books, and didn't have corroborating bank slips, receipts or records of transactions.

- Altermeds opening inventory each year for three consecutive years was $0 (as if they had sold everything on hand by December 31st at midnight).
- The end of the second year showed over $12,000 in inventory, but there was no record of how any costs were assigned to units of inventory.
- Their 1040 Schedule C, "profit or loss from business" showed that they selected the Cash Method of Accounting (Accrual is required for proper cost accounting).
- The court held that Altermeds selling non-marijuana merchandise was not separate from the business of selling marijuana merchandise. NOTE: If, however, selling non-marijuana merchandise was considered a separate business, then the expenses of that business would be deductible. See CHAMP, 128 T.C. at 183-185.

CHAPTER 18 – IRS CASH FORM 8300 AND BANK SECRECY ACT

A known IRS audit trigger for cannabis companies has been the failure to timely file IRS Form 8300. It's more intricate than simply filing a Form 8300 when you receive $10,000 or more in cash at once.

Colorado's cannabis industry found out the importance of timely filing these puppies the hard way. The IRS has instituted CIP (Compliance Initiative Projects) which are any projects designed to identify, measure, or analyze taxpayer noncompliance. They study or analyze groups of individuals, businesses, specific occupations, industries, geographic areas or specific economic activities or events. You guessed it, they are gathering data and using it to analyze tax compliance. The IRS scrutinized the Colorado cannabis industry to identify those failing to properly file 8300's which became the jumping off point for audits. Rumor has it that there is a similar IRS initiative in California at present. We spoke with an accountant for a client's distributor in the Bay Area just last week, who told us that "nobody in California files 8300's because they would have to do them all the time." We reminded him that inconvenience doesn't change federal law.

Form 8300 is used to report the receipt of payments of more than $10,000 that are comprised of any combination of U.S. currency, foreign currency, cashier's checks, money orders, bank drafts and traveler's checks – basically cash. We will go straight to the IRS for the type of payments to report:

Trades and businesses must report cash payments received if all of the following criteria are met:

1. The amount of cash is more than $10,000
2. The business receives the cash as:
   - One lump sum of more than $10,000, or
   - Installment payments that cause the total cash received within one year of the initial payment to total more than $10,000, or
   - Previously unreported payments that cause the total cash received within a 12-month period to total more than $10,000
3. The establishment receives the cash in the ordinary course of a trade or business
4. The same agent or buyer provides the cash
5. The business receives the cash in a single transaction or in related transactions

You must also complete a single Form 8300 and treat two or more transactions with the same party as a single transaction if they total $10,000 or more and occur within a 24 hours period.

The purpose of the form is to help authorities detect illegal activities such as money laundering, tax evasion, terrorism, etc. The form can be found on the IRS's website – ensure you are using the current revision, the most recent is 2014: https://www.irs.gov/pub/irs-pdf/f8300.pdf.

You must file within 15 days of receipt of the payment(s) and can do so online via the BSA E-Filing System of the Financial Crimes Enforcement Network (a.k.a. FinCEN). Here is the link: https://bsaefiling.fincen.treas.gov/main.html.

After filing a Form 8300, you must start a new cash count of payments from that buyer and if they total more than $10,000 over the next 12 months, you must file another Form 8300. You are required to keep a copy of Form 8300 for at least 5 years and there are stiff penalties for not timely filing or including all required information, starting at $250 per incident (for errors with a single

Form 8300) and climbing depending upon the circumstances. You may also be subject to criminal penalties for willfully failing to adhere to the filing requirements, which can include prison time and massive fines. If you correct your negligence on Form 8300 within 30 days of its due date, the penalty drops to $50, and if fixed after the 30th day but by August 1st, the penalty is reduced to $100.

Form 8300, line 1 has a checkbox for a "suspicious transaction." The receiver of cash can voluntarily fill out this form even if the amount does not exceed $10,000. A suspicious transaction is defined as "…a transaction in which it appears that a person is attempting to cause Form 8300 not to be filed, or to file a false or incomplete form." If a transaction is $9,900 at noon on Friday, then at 12:01 PM on Saturday the same party initiates another $9,900 transaction, it is quite apparent that they are avoiding Form 8300. You may want to check the box (or consult with your attorney as we aren't giving legal advice), because otherwise you may be complicit in this "structuring" of transactions to avoid Form 8300 and may be subject to civil and criminal penalties. Structuring could be any amount as long as the intent to avoid the Form 8300 is present.

The BSA in "BSA E-Filing System of FinCEN" stands for Bank Secrecy Act. Banks are not required to fill out form 8300 as they adhere to stricter guidelines, which not only require the reporting of over $10,000, but require banks to report "suspicious activity" and "structuring." Banks are required to maintain an internal log of cash transactions of more than $3,000 so they can identify suspicious activity per these requirements.

IMPORTANT NOTE: On or before Jan. 31 of the following year, you must provide to the customer who gave you the cash a statement with the following information:

- The name and address of the cash recipient's business.
- Name and telephone number of a contact person for the business.
- The total amount of reportable cash received in a 12- month period, and
- A statement that the cash recipient is reporting the information to the IRS.

If you are routinely involved in large cash transactions, you will want to get familiar with the IRS's Form 8300 Reference Guide for more detailed guidance: https://www.irs.gov/businesses/smallbusinesses-self-employed/irs-form-8300-reference-guide.

CHAPTER 19 – CASH AND BANKING

As you know, banking is an immense challenge in this industry. There are solutions, but they come with a price in the form of up-front fees to screen applicants and then a hefty percentage of deposits as well as armored car fees to transport cash. Many industry participants are setting up bank accounts for holding or management companies, etc. and not disclosing to the bank the nature of their business. This often leads to bank accounts being closed. Sneaking money into a bank account just doesn't work and may border on fraud in some instances. One thing is for certain, if you are going to pony up and get a "real" bank account, the compliance work that the bank requires will entail a hard look at the source of your funds. This is another instance where having your records and financial statements in order is a must. Some banks will even take legacy cash if it is documented on financial statements.

Did you know you can also pay your federal taxes with cash? Up to $1,000 per day will be accepted for a $4 fee at thousands of locations using PayNearMe (available in most states). Here's a link: https://www.officialpayments.com/fed/index.jsp.

GREEN BEAN CFO

Please send any feedback or requests for topics to be covered in the updated version to the author, Brian@GreenBeanCFO.com or give him a call at 508.889.9785.

To request more information simply email info@GreenBeanCFO.com

If you are looking for cannabis-specific marketing email Brandon@GreenBeanCFO.com.

Follow us on IG, where cannabis lives. @GreenBeanCFO @GreenBeanMKTG

Visit GreenBeanCFO.com for regular updates and blog posts.

Thank you for sticking with us through this book. We wish you nothing but green pastures in all your cannabis endeavors!

Made in the USA
Coppell, TX
13 June 2020

28002308R10066